SOCIAL SCIENCES DIVISION
CHICAGO PUBLIC LIBRARY
400 SOUTH STATE STREET
CHICAGO, IL 60605

X

CHICAGO PUBLIC LIBRARY

S0-ANN-553

LA217
.H 793
1986
Cop 1

SOCIAL SCIENCES DIVISION
CHICAGO PUBLIC LIBRARY
400 SOUTH STATE STREET
CHICAGO, IL 60605

THE CHICAGO PUBLIC LIBRARY

11.16

DEMCO

AMERICAN EDUCATION:

Let's Cut the Yarn

by

John J. Hunt

ETC Publications

LA 217
.H 793
1986
cop1

C | **P**

Library of Congress Cataloging-in-Publication Data

Hunt, John J., 1935-
    American public education.

    1. Public schools—United States.   2. Education—
United States—Aims and objectives.   3. Education—United
States—Finance.   I. Title.
LA217.H793 1986   371^1.01^{1}0973   85-13170
ISBN 0-88280-113-9

No part of this publication may be reproduced or transmitted
in any form or by any means, electronic or mechanical,
including photocopy, recording, or any information storage
and retrieval system known or to be invented, without
permission in writing from the publisher, except by a reviewer
who wishes to quote brief passages in connection with a review
written for inclusion in a magazine, periodical, newspaper, or
broadcast.

Copyright © 1986 by John J. Hunt

Published by ETC Publications
Palm Springs
California 92263

All rights reserved

Printed in the United States of America

OCIAL SCIENCES DIVISION
CHICAGO PUBLIC LIBRARY
400 SOUTH STATE STREET
CHICAGO, IL 60605

ACKNOWLEDGMENTS

This is the page given to the author on which he identifies those to whom he wishes to say "thanks." If anyone reading this page does not find his/her name and feels piqued, then you know you are one to whom I owe a sincere "thanks."

I intend to acknowledge three institutions and one person.

First, the institution of peanut butter, second, the institution of jelly and third, Vanderbilt University (more precisely, Peabody at Vanderbilt). It is these three great American institutions which sustained me.

The one person I wish to acknowledge is Lint Deck (more precisely, Dr. L. Linton Deck, Jr.; Chairman, Department of Educational Leadership, Peabody at Vanderbilt). I cite him for his wit, brain, courage, humor and heart, most especially his heart. Lint is a sucker for struggling graduate students, stray dogs and singlehanded sailors. Thank heavens there is so little difference between stray dogs and singlehanded sailors.

TABLE OF CONTENTS

INTRODUCTION

Some years ago there was a country music song in which the singer described his everyday going-to-work routine. He sang of how he drove from his house the same time each morning to the main highway, turned right and joined the many others driving to work. On some mornings when the highway traffic was heavy, the singer had time to look across the main highway and observe how the secondary road he was on turned to gravel, then to a meandering path and finally blended into the farm field alongside the seabound river. He always turned right and went to work. But he dreamed of one day crossing the highway instead of turning right. He never did, but he dreamed of it in song.

In 1983, after talking it over with and gaining the agreement of my wife, I decided that fourteen months later I would cross the highway to the path and follow the river to the sea. On March 10, 1984 I brought the mooring lines aboard my 31-foot sailboat and followed the Dog River, to Mobile Bay, to the Gulf of Mexico, to the Atlantic Ocean.

The agreement with my wife was simple. I'd quit my job and take 6-months doing what I always wanted to do. After my return and re-employment, Sue would quit her job and take 6-months doing what she had always wanted to do.

Ten thousand four hundred and thirty ocean miles and 6-months later I reset the mooring lines from my boat to the dock in Dog River. This is not a story of my wanderings, mostly alone, across the Atlantic twice and east coast of our country; rather, it's the reduction to paper of the recurring thougths about the business I had left behind: American Public Education.

You see, I quit one of the very highly esteemed school superintendencies to go sailing. I had been a superintendent of schools for fifteen years, first in New Jersey then in Arizona and finally, in a forty-eight thousand student county school district in Alabama. When I left I was the chief executive officer of a seventy-plus million dollar yearly operating budget and an organization employing upwards of four thousand adults.

I must confess, in all the ten-thousand miles, I never once thought about superintending. After investing so many years into the job, I never missed it. Harry Truman's adage prevailed, "Don't Look Back." What I did think about was the "business," i.e., American Public Education.

For some reason I've not fathomed, I did not think about a particular job. I did think, for example, about my undergraduate years as an engineering student and atehlete at Princeton, my years as an aviator and Marine, my years as a math teacher and coach, and my years as a graduate student at Harvard and my short post-doctoral summer at Stanford, but never about any *one* job.

Consequently, what I write here is not about Alabama particularly, nor Arizona, nor New Jersey, nor New York, nor any of the regions in which we've had the good fortune to live and raise our family these past twenty-five years. It's about American Public Schools, the "business" of public education in our country. And believe me, when it gets to consuming seventy-million in one place and seventy-billion dollars all over the place, it's a business. It's a close-to-the-heart enterprise because it's our children and our country's future, but I promise you, it's a business.

What I have to say about our American Public Education seems very clear to me after ten-thousand miles and, if you'll pardon my sailor's tongue, very simply stated: We must "cut the yarn" in our public education. Now . . . we must do it now . . not twenty-five years from now, but now. If we don't do it now, we will be a second-rate society in twenty-five years, a third-rate society in fifty years and, the way things are moving in education in other countries, within a hundred years we will be an historical example of another grandiose Republican experiment in democracy that failed; just like the Greeks. Two hundred years from now tourists will visit our captial just as we visit the Parthenon these days and wonder at a society lost.

"What's yarn?" you ask. In the years before plastics, ropes were made from yarn. On trips lasting sometimes years the sailors had to make the ship's rope. They would sit around in a group and hand roll yarn into line. Woven lines became rope. While sitting around working the yarn the sailors would tell stories much as campers do around the campfire. Good story tellers could hold a group spellbound for hours. As the teller wove the story further and further away from reality and fact it became a "yarn." Cowboys around a campfire on the range would call it "bull....." This book would have never gotten to print if I had gone off wrangling.

Unless we "cut the yarn" surrounding American Public Education now, our society will simply be a lesson to the students of some other society. We will be an example of how an entire democratic society can decay for want of a sound, universal, free education system so fundamental to any society, on any planet in this universe. That's my grandchildren, probably your great-grandchildren, we're talking about here. We're not talking about somebody else's society, somebody else's flesh and blood. We're talking about *our* flesh and blood only a generation or two removed.

Unless we cut the yarn now we will assure that our greatgrandchildren will be scratching out a living for the enjoyment and good life of others in some other society. Our flesh and blood will be hoping someday to emigrate *out* of the USA to a first-rate country.

"Why?" because you and I sealed our grandchildrens' fate way back there in the 1980's. If there's a sailor alive somewhere then, he'll probably sum us up succinctly by observing, "All they did was yarn 'bout it. They never cut the yarnin' and did somethin' before it was too late."

"How late is it?" Let's think back. Before World War II most education around our planet was "privileged" as compared to "universal." In most countries education was bought by the family, not paid for by taxes. Except of course, in our country. In Japan, Germany, and Russia, just to name a few countries, education was bought by the family. Education was mostly for the privileged. What little tax-supported schooling that did exist was mainly to train workers and sort out the few highly intelligent peasants' children useable by the privileged.

Whole society's were obliterated in that war. Not only did nations have to rebuild bricks and mortar, they had to rebuild societies. What, after World War II, was a distinctive characteristic of the victor's society? Universal free public education. Not only did our cigarette lighters, transistor radios and automobiles get copied, our concept of education got copied. And, like our autos, radios, and lighters, the copies were improved versions of the original.

At the end of that planet-wide convulsion our country had an educational advantage. The gap between our free universal public education system and the systems of education for the privileged was as large as the gap between the societies of the vanquished and the victor.

But, from that time on the gap began to narrow. We had a distinct societal advantage when we were the only ones with the A-bomb and the only ones with free, public, universal education. Both situations have changed these past forty years. Everyone recognizes the nuclear change. Few seem to recognize the educational change. What's worse, we've still got the same educational system we had in '44 (with some few exceptions) while much of the rest of the planet now has the updated, improved copy. Wouldn't we be in one hell of a fix if we were trying to maintain our military defenses with the same A-bombs we had in '44? However they got it, other nations copied and improved upon what we had as a nuclear arsenal.

The same holds true for our primary fundamental societal defense, education. Other nations copied and improved upon what we had. The difference, however, is that we are still trying to maintain our '44 education arsenal. The gap, the advantage we had is gone.

Nobody yarned, "Let's continue using those propellar driven bombers because they're a great American tradition." Why then have we said it and done it in education? We may have parity in modern nuclear destructive capacity but we're in one hell of a fix when it comes to our fundamental *constructive* capacity.

John J. Hunt
Apollo Beach, Florida

I

A LOOK BACK AT OUR WAKE
(Known Otherwise As An Historical View)

Let's just look back for one short minute, nothing heavy, no dates, no footnotes, nothing of that kind; just a quick look back over our shoulder. That's all it takes to look back to the beginning of our grand experiment, and from there up to the present; just a quick glance. We've been around, as a society for so short a time, measured in ticks of the universal clock, that it only takes a quick glance to take in all of our history.

Our history only goes back about 200 years. Hell, that's nothing (there goes my sailor's tongue again, I'll try and curb it.) For example, my little boat leaves a track in the ocean about one boat-length (31-feet) behind it as it plows through the ocean. The Atlantic Ocean route I took was 3,600 miles long. The length of the ocean surface disturbance I made, we made—I and my boat—was nothing, compared to the expanse of the ocean.

Our track as a nation, as a society, when compared to the expanse of time, is the equivalent of about one boat-length of wake; nothing. We are so young as a nation we have barely scratched the expanse of time. If we sank in the next 200 years, we would have been nearly nothing as a society . . . our trace would be gone in another tick of universal time.

In short, the most that can be said of us at this time is that we, our Republican democracy, is a "promising experiment." If we sink, that's all we will have been, a short-lived experiment in the total expanse of time.

If we succeed, my oh my, if we succeed, things will never ever be the same on this planet. Time will well record our wake if we succeed.

And we *are* an experiment, make no mistake about it, we are *the* human social experiment. At a time when it's fashionable for many of my Princeton and Harvard contemporaries to be detractors, let's you and I not forget, we are part of the grandest, the damndest experiment to come along on the surface of time. Who in God's creation ever imagined a society of laws? Before our experiment the rule was "might," he with the biggest gun ruled (or with the most money to buy the biggest guns, it's the same.)

Who would ever have thought 200 million people would live together under the rule of "law," whatever that is. You can't pick up the law, put a shell in its chamber and aim it at somebody to convince him to do what you want. And yet you and I do a hundred things a day because "it's the law."

10

Who would ever believe that every four years or so the most powerful man in the world would voluntarily hand over all of his power to another—voluntarily—simply because it's the "law." We've done it 37 or 38 times now.

The Russians have yet to do it once. They'll let the guy stay in the position until he dies rather than try an orderly, peaceable transfer of power. When you think of it, the Russians do only what the Romans did, it's what the Asian dynastys did: *we* are the experiment, not they.

We are a nation of "laws." And what wonderful laws they are! Freedoms of press, speech, assembly, religion, *et al*. Definitely the greatest experiment this planet has ever seen.

Now, there're a few items you've got to have if this experiment is to work. Jefferson saw it right off, back at the very beginning. One of those items is what he called an "enlightened democracy." You've got to have people who can read those laws, write those laws and, most importantly, appreciate "law," the rule of law, enough to agree, voluntarily to live by it; and die for it!

Jefferson knew it. For this grand experiment to work *all* the people in the experiment must be able to read, write, discuss, argue and understand, think and act, create and change; in short everybody has to be educated. And the governments has to see to it. Jefferson said that right off. (In better than sailor's words, of course) Everybody, not just the rich; not just the males; not just whites: everybody. Otherwise the experiment won't last long enough for the ink to dry on the Bill of Rights and the Constitution. Without an educated society, we won't last on the surface of time any longer than my boat's wake lasts on the ocean.

Our short minute is up. We've looked back long enough. Let's look down now, right alongside the boat where the wake is being made. Do you see 1929? That's so close to us in time it's not even behind the boat yet. Remember 1929? The stockmarket crashed, people jumped from office building windows; a substantial portion of the nation was flat broke. Remember?

I can tell you something about 1929 I'll bet you don't remember. During all those years of bone-crushing national poverty we, our nation, never shut down the schools. Oh, we shortened some school years, paid some teachers on credit, things of that sort, but despite the little money we had as a nation we never shut down our public schools. Right through the entire depression our nation's schools remained open and free. Banks closed, businesses failed, apples cost a nickle and people starved; but their children went to school.

Look there at the 1940's, just "yesterday." We fought a planet-wide war. We were on the ropes at times in that war. We were in desperate need of guns, tanks, ships and other war machinery. Our factories ran 'round the clock. We could easily have doubled our production had we closed our high schools and put students to work in the war factories. Did we? We did not. We wouldn't even take people into the Army until they were past high-school age.

In the 1930's many of our grandparents literally went hungry, but their children went to school. In the 1940's many of our parents literally died for want of more armaments but their kids went to school.

O.K., now we can look up. We're done with history. We know how much our founders valued education, we know how much our grandparents valued it, we know how much our parents valued it for all of us.

Now I ask you, right here and now on the surface of time, don't you think we ought to cut the yarnin' about education? You know and I know that we don't want to be the ones about whom it is written "The experiment failed because they couldn't spare the dime?" It's time for you and me to cut the yarn surrounding free public education for all; it's time we started supporting it with money, not "yarn."

"Not me," you say. "I'm retired."

"Not me, I don't have any kids."

Friend, let me ask you a question. Do you like your social security? Are you looking forward to retirement? Somebody's got to be working to pay for your social security check. You are weaving wool around your head if you think a grape-picker in a decaying society can earn enough money to pay his/her share of your social security. They will emigrate first. Cut the yarn, friend, you've got a bigger interest in a healthy public education system than most. You want those kiddies to grow up with a good education so they can earn a good buck 'cause you'll get part of it. All you'll get is grapes if the kid's earning yen.

Our fathers, grandmothers and great-grandparents knew quite clearly what free universal public education meant to the USA. They knew what a good education would mean to their children. They knew, perhaps because the alternative was closer to their recollection, what the public schools meant to their new country; what schools meant to the grand experiment.

Do we know? We yarn that we do. But, let's compare our actions to our words. Retired people vote down tax proposals for public education and then go around *proudly* proclaiming another victory for "grey power." As kids that kind of foolish behavior would have gotten a good thrashing. Working people without kids yarn that it's not their problem. They don't have kids so they don't have to worry. They, of course, don't have to worry; until the company they work for shuts down and the job they had moves to Japan because some smart Japanese has figured out how to do the job with a robot. Parents with kids of their own, they'll make sure their kids get the education they need even if mother has to work full-time to earn the tuition so the child can attend a "good" school with the privileged. To hell with the rest. And the rest of us. We don't care because we've never had an education. Let's stop the yarnin'.

II

IMPRESSMENT DON'T WORK
(Known Otherwise As "You Get What You Pay For.")

Back in the "old days," when slavery was "in" onshore, "impressment" was the equivalent at sea. A ship needed a crew to work its sails to make it go. The ship's first mate would pick a dark night, pay the local constable to stay home, and go into town looking for crew. When he found a drunk, or even a family man hurrying home alone in the dark, the first mate would apply the belaying pin to the back of the head and the guy would wake up the next morning at sea. If the guy wanted to eat, he had to work. He was what they called "impressed." If the new sailor still bucked, there was always the cat-o-nine tails . . . very impressive.

Impressment doesn't work any more at sea. It doesn't work in public education either. People simply leave the first chance they get—ships and schools. If you want a crew these days, you've got to pay them. If you want a good ship that goes well and earns a good return on investment, you've got to pay the crew well. In the merchant marine business, you get what you pay for. It's exactly the same in the education business, you get what you pay for.

Don't tell me about a "calling," either to the sea or to teaching. Business is business. You want good people to work for you? Then you're going to have to pay them.

Don't let me mislead you. You can always get bodies. You can even get live bodies that will kiss your hand and tell you how much they just *love* their calling. They're yarnin' you, friend, it's the best they can get. You're going to end up with leaky boats and foundering schools.

The one, simple, bedrock fundamental fact stares us in the face if we cut the yarn. Good teachers make good schools. To get good teachers you've got to pay good money.

"What ever happened to the good old days?" you ask. "When I was in school Mrs. Smith was the best teacher there could ever be, a tough disciplinarian who cared about me. She made less money than teachers make now, had a larger class size and rough ruffians to keep in line. Nobody fooled with Mrs. Smith, she had eyes in the back of her head."

I hate to be the bearer of bad news but Mrs. Smith is gone—for good. Mrs. Smith was making low wages then and you may wistfully wish to recreate the good old days but they're gone. Back in those days Mrs. Smith worked as a teacher because most other career avenues for an intelligent female college graduate were closed. In short, schools had a high quality captive workforce:

women. Nowadays Ms. Smith is a bank vice president earning the kind of money someone of her brains and drive deserves. Schools no longer have a captive minority to draw from.

To get Ms. Smith these days the schools have to compete with the bank, or wherever the Ms. Smiths are knocking down barriers. God bless 'em. And the original dedicated Mrs. Smith you remember? Let's cut the yarn. Had Mrs. Smith not been the object of discrimination, she'd have jumped ship in the bat of an eye and ended up owning that bank. But, high quality Mrs. Smith demonstrated to us all what a high-caliber teacher can do. She taught us well. A good teacher will do all that Mrs. Smith did then, and more. But, we will have to pay for that teacher now and, unless impressment or slavery returns, we'll have to pay to get that quality "evermore."

"The salary for a teacher these days isn't that bad, for a nine-month job," you say. Now you're yarnin' me.

Two jobs, we'll compare them. Job one pays $15,000 per year for 185 days of work. Job two pays $21,500 per year for 250 days of work. All else is the same, work conditions, benefits (they aren't, the 250 day job's are almost always better but we'll pass on that for now); consider all else equal. Which job would you take straight out of college? Don't yarn me my good friend, you're not dumb. I know damn well which job you'd take.

The same two jobs, five years later. Your college roommate was not as smart as you and took the $15,000 job, expecting to travel in the off months. Now it's five years later. With the annual $250 increments and *two 15* percent salary increases your roommate is making $19,305 per year. (Obviously I'm bending backwards to make this comparison fair.)

In the same five years you've done an average job, getting eight percent raises three out of the five years. One year times were tough and nobody got a raise, the other year you did poorly and got no raise. You are making $27,082 a year. Your company decides to expand and adds another position just like yours, advertising for someone with five years work experience for $25,000 per year (an equal opportunity employer of course). Guess who is going to jump for your company's job?

Now let's just crank in a little of that good old fashioned yarn-free reality. Your company has a better benefit package, a better retirement package and better working conditions, which is generally the case. You know your roommate is going to jump ship. Your roommate was not dumb.

But nonetheless, let's say your roommate listens to all your hard facts-of-life arguments and still decides to stay on in job one. "I like the kids," is the answer. Or worse, "Conditions are going to improve, the new governor made us the promise during his campaign."

Very soon you're both 40 years old and each with two kids nearing college age; average kids, no athletic or academic scholarships likely. You may grumble about the costs but you can afford to pay for your kid's college. Your roommate, on the other hand has been a teacher all this time, cannot afford the children's college education costs. The teacher's annual salary is now barely half yours. The teacher has to moonlight.

"Tough," you say. "My roommate made his/her bed, now it's time to sleep in it." Ah, but your younger child is about to enter the high school class taught by a college graduate who can't even afford to send his own kids to college; a situation not unlike your roommate's. You attend parents' night, meet the teacher and come away wondering if you did, in fact, detect some sourness behind the teacher's eyes or in the teacher's voice.

Cut the yarn. You know damn well you saw bitterness. You saw somebody going through the motions. You recoginzed it all right, you just fear facing up to it. You're about to get what you paid for.

Quite simply, the position of teacher in our society must rise. Teachers must occupy a higher position in our economic pecking order. As it is now, the prospects, to a college student, of becoming a teacher are dismal. We discourage quality from ever entering the career. A college kid looks at the starting salaries for teachers, as compared to almost all other career possibilities, and heads for something else. We don't stop there. In the first five years of a teaching career we drive out another substantial portion of quality from teaching, in the second five years we promote another sizeable portion out. By year fifteen we have some good teachers remaining, generally a second-income family member or a teacher whose moonlight job has turned lucrative and couldn't be continued easily except from a teaching slot, or a few altruists. We have another group doing satisfactorily with a minimum of effort, the soured. And we have a group of weak teachers who have settled in. Each of these types of teachers have, after 15 years, at least 25 more years of teaching 'til retirement; 25 years with little prospect of any substantial income improvement.

The remedies tried so far have usually been punitive. "Root the baggage out" type laws exist in every state. These laws don't work except in the very extreme case (molesters, felons, etc.) and, even if these laws did work, with what would we be replacing the settled-in weak teachers? More of the same, the sequence of events would simply cycle-in the next group with all the same characteristics.

The quality of teaching is not going to improve by improving the punitive laws. Without wasting your time here on a legal diatribe, believe me, a tenured teacher has a "property right" to his/her tenured position. Removing one's property right under the law is an intricate, time-consuming, expensive process. It can be done but the judicial protections for the property owner make the "Miranda" requirements look kindergartenish. And when it's all done and the lawyers have their fees and the administrator has been vilified as we'll discuss later, what've we got? We've got blood all over the barroom floor and many people resolving never to go through that again; people deciding it's easier to cope. We do not have improved teaching, or weak teachers working to improve because they're running scared, which is the theory behind punitive laws. We have more people trying to cope, that's all we have.

We could remove tenure, but, by that time we'd have the problem of teaching in sub-arctic cold because hell would have frozen over.

There are other solutions. We don't even have to come up with an original idea. We can copy from countries who originally copied from us. Japan, for example, simply raised all teachers salaries a few years ago by 20-percent. The position of teacher in the Japanese social pecking order was seen to be falling so *all* teachers' salaries were raised overnite, by 20-percent.

"We can't do that," you say. "We have no centralized educational system," you say. We don't have a centralized educational system, with that much authority I'll agree, but we can do it. When we in this country have a mind to do something, we do it. We find a way short of disrupting the entire structure of the country.

When we finally wanted to stop the George Maddoxes from discriminating in their restaurants against citizens with black skin we hooked a little old rider to the interstate commerce laws. Anybody involved in interstate commerce could not discriminate on the basis of race, creed, color, religion, or national origin. George, it turns out, had things in his restaurant purchased out-of-state; i.e., he was involved in interstate commerce and therefore had to stop that discrimination foolishness.

When we have a mind to do something in this country, we find a way.

There is a way to move the teaching position up the social pecking order into the middle of the middle class where we've got to have it in order to attract higher caliber people to teaching. We can use our tax policies.

We've used our tax policies to improve our national energy position by giving write-offs to oil prospectors, we use our tax policies to sustain our universities by making gifts tax deductible; we've even used our tax policies to improve our defense of America's cup. (I'll bet you didn't know that! Those wealthy people sailing those expensive boats off Newport are working off tax deductions and non-taxable donations to non-profit front corporations.) There are, literally, thousands of examples of the use of our federal tax policies to advance a national need or solve a national problem. We can do it for the teaching position.

Were we to say in our federal tax laws that income earned from public school teaching was not taxible we would move the position of teacher up the social and economic pecking order very quickly and simply.

Listen to the outcries. "We've never used our tax policies to give any one portion of our society such an advantage." "It would cost too much." "If we do it for teachers, we'd have to do it for police, state workers, firemen and everybody else on the public payroll." Listen to the yarn.

Our tax policies do give certain of our number an advantage. You know that to be the case. There's nothing particularly wrong with the idea as long as there's a national interest being met. The tax policies for farmers are a good example.

It would not cost "too" much. For three million public school teachers to be forgiven federal taxes on income from teaching up to three times the household poverty level, it would reduce federal revenues by 14 billion dollars per year. I don't mean to be smart about this but that much money falls off the lunch counter in the Pentagon in one day.

We wouldn't have to create a new federal bureaucracy to accomplish this. We wouldn't have to establish a new cabinet position. We wouldn't have overhead. The IRS is already there.

I'm not finished. Let's look at the benefit package problem. Medical insurance people are ruthlessly driving the teacher further down the economic and social pecking ladder. Remove the teaching position from this trap of low to middle income families unable to risk a major medical bill and therefore paying a larger and larger portion of their limited income into health insurance. Provide full medical coverage for teachers and teachers' families through the Veteran's Hospital system.

As a by-product, we'd have an improved Veteran's Hospital system for veterans. Something needed desperately. The federal government owns that hospital system now. It stretches and contracts in size from war to peace to war. Rapid spasms of size always wreck havoc in organizations of any kind. A system with a more size-stable population to serve can function far more efficiently . . . equipment and employees are then more cost effective. It's another federal bureaucracy all ready, and in place which would minimize overhead costs. And, as strange as this sounds, the "readiness" of the Veterans Hospital system for war would be improved.

As things stand now, the VA hospitals have to

scramble to enlarge rapidly. They have to draw people in a hurry; taking, at times, anybody they can get who qualifies. A larger, more size-stable group of medical employees could be employed into the VA Hospitals if the population served was larger and more consistent in size. At a cost equivalent to 75 dollars per month per teacher, the three-million teachers would require a VA Hospital budget increase of 2.7 billion dollars.

I know, I know, as Sam Rayburn said, "A billion here and a billion there and pretty soon it adds up to real money." The loss of federal revenue and the added federal expense, taken together, would amount to 17 billion current dollars.

And say "no" to the fireman, policeman, and state civil servant. Our problem now is other societies on this planet are out distancing us in the most fundamental societal need—education.

These two measures would relieve the average teacher's annual revenue by approximately $5,500 of "load." Remember your roommate after five years in a teaching career? There was an $8,000 difference between you two. These two actions would close that gap and put your roommate into the social economic pecking order at about the same place as you . . . perhaps a little lower still. Had these two items been on the books when you and your roommate graduated, both of you might have gone into teaching.

I'm still not finished with this topic of impressment and slavery. There's still that thorny problem of college costs for the middle-aged teacher. I'd venture to say it's the one, single most souring factor for the middle-aged teacher. The teacher's been providing education to other people's children for 20 years and finds he/she can't provide it to his/her own kids when they come up to college age.

A hundred or so years ago federal law set aside federal land (1/16th of every section) the revenue from which was to create "Land Grant Colleges." (What a grand experiment this Republican democracy is!) That law still holds. Let's modify it to add a clause that says the children of every public school teacher, resident and teaching in the state the previous five years, shall attend that state's land-grant college free: room, board, tuition, books, the works. This makes education a benefit for educators.

Again, no new bureaucracy needed; little or no overhead involved. If ten-percent of the three-million teachers in our example have college kids and land-grant college costs are four thousand dollars per year, it might cost a state 24 million dollars in tuition revenue. It would lift a $4,000 "load" off the middle-aged teacher's revenue.

Now we've got the position of teacher smack dab in the middle of the socio-economic pecking order, right in the middle of the middle class.

These three items, use of federal taxing policy, federal medical programs and state land-grant colleges are, from all I can find, legal, feasible and practical. The teaching position would become, if not more attractive, at least equally as attractive as other middle-class career positions.

Public education would have a fighting chance to attract you and your roommate into teaching careers. More importantly, Ms. Smith might even come back, and that's no yarn.

III

OBSERVING AND EVALUATING TEACHERS
(Or Harry Truman Was Only Partly Right)

It is said that Harry Truman had a sign in the Oval Office when he was President which read, "The Buck Stops Here." If Harry meant to imply that the power rested where the "yes/no" authority rested, he was only partly right.

There's more to power than authority. There is, for example, the bureaucratic power to delay or divert the "buck" bound for Harry's desk. This capability to slow down, divert, or even facilitate a request for approval is developed into a fine art by successful bureaucrats. It's one of the reasons we all complain about "red-tape" when we become involved with any of the many bureaucracies which affect us. Were you, or I, to make a request of a governmental agency we very likely would become frustrated by the time and effort it takes to get an answer. Our request may seem to us perfectly straightforward and not the least bit out of the ordinary. It's just that our request begins to resemble a power chip in the internal bureaucratic game. Our request gets slowed or moved along its way for reasons quite unrelated to its substance.

If Harry found himself worried and weighted down by the heavy decisions he had to make, he should also have been equally as worried by the decisions he should have been making but wasn't because they weren't getting to his desk; decisions caught in the bureaucracy's power game. Having read much of what's been written about Harry Truman, I'm inclined to think he did attend to his bureaucratic homework and saw to it he had his "expediters" along the request route, seeing to it things got done; or things he wanted done got done (Harry was as crafty as anybody). I wonder if his facilitators were called principals.

That's what principals are these days in school organizations. The principal is the linchpin among the interlocking wheels and gears inside a bureaucracy. When the linchpin fits properly everything moves along smoothly and the organization achieves its task. A principal can obfuscate or expedite matters. An incompetent principal merely obfuscates and "snafu's" things because she/he knows no better. An accomplished principal obfuscates or expedites according to the internal power game, expediting that which will improve her/his power position and obfuscating anything which will subtract from her/his power. (I'm sorry about that word "obfuscate" but it's the nearest legitimate word to the word I'd like to use.)

Of course, the bureaucratic power game is much

more sophisticated than I've portrayed it. A player in the game works to advance his/her position, usually at the expense of another player. A question, issue, or request is routed, expedited, or slowed according to the impact it might have upon another's power, or another coalition's power, etc. Power is a very interesting topic in and of itself when it comes to understanding formal and informal organizational structures, but that's not our topic here. Teaching is our topic.

The point I want to make about the principal is this: a crafty, accomplished principal can actually improve his power position (and, hence, his/her longevity) by obfuscating the process of observing teachers. As a matter of fact, the principal position is the only $30,000 + position I know of in which the less one does of the critical responsibility to observe and evaluate subordinates, the longer one stays in the post.

Evaluating causes hassles, hassles cause disorder, and order is a bureaucracy's oxygen. Evaluate subordinates properly and eventually one's going to uncover an incompetent subordinate. The incompetent subordinate's union starts to stir, the community starts to stir, unrest raises its head and suddenly there's a disquieting disorder where orderliness used to be. A crafty, accomplished principal stays out of this kind of pickle. And the marginal teacher stays on.

Consequently, the crafty principal does only as much observing and evaluating of teachers as is required by contract . . . and then does it with all the drama of an adolescent mowing the lawn because it's required of him/her. When and only when a subordinate's incompetence threatens orderliness is he/she hidden, or transferred, or pressured out, or entrapped and given the option of resigning quietly; but only when the incompetence threatens the orderliness of the situation.

The less one does of this "messy" business of evaluating and observing and improving instruction, the better off one is as a principal.

There is a disclaimer which has to go here. I have had some really masterful principals who "got rid of" incompetent, marginal and even average subordinates without so much as a ripple on the calm of the school's peaceful orderliness. There may have been something less than full regard for the individual subordinate's rights to due process, but the net result was a "good" and high achieving school. There are such principals but they are too rare to move sufficient numbers of our schools to the effectiveness level we need.

The average ordinary of us in public schools are just that: average and ordinary. We operate in bureaucracies just as average ordinary people in other bureaucracies operate. We sustain ourselves. We might tell you otherwise, but you should recognize that by now it's yarn. To move the effectiveness level of a bureaucracy to a higher level, it's the preponderant average which has to be motivated to move; motivated, not forced.

In nearly every school in this nation there exists a "law" of some sort (state law, school board policy, contract term, etc.) requiring the principal to evaluate each non-tenured teacher each year. Usually some portion of the tenured teaching staff is also evaluated each year. For example, a principal typically may be required to observe each non-tenured teacher each year and one-third of the tenured staff.

Let's say it's a 2000 pupil high school with 100 teachers, 20 percent of whom are non-tenured. Typically, the principal would have to do 20 classroom observations for the non-tenured, one each, and 17 more observations of tenured teachers, one-third of the tenured staff, each year. In other words, the principal in our example will have done about 37 (20 + 17) classroom observations in a 180 day school year, about once every five school days on the average. An observation typically lasts half an hour, the subsequent conference with the teacher and paperwork is another half hour; one hour per observation is average. But, just to be on the fair side in this case, let's double the time and consider each observation consumes two hours.

At two hours per observation the principal in our example would spend 74 hours of the school year in activities directly related to the observation of classroom teaching, i.e., 37 observation/evaluation activities lasting two hours each. That's not an unusual load for a 2,000 pupil high school for the principal.

Don't for a minute think the principal is sitting sipping coffee for all the other hours of a school year. She/he is seldom even standing still, if any good at the job. I'm not trying to portray a principal's job as easy or principals as loafers. A good principal is plenty busy. It's not whether the principal's day is full, it is. It's a question of what fills the principal's day, or, more accurately, what *does not* fill the principal's time.

What does not fill the principal's day is classroom observation of teachers teaching. Teaching five one-hour periods per day in a 180-day school year, a teacher teaches for 900 hours. If the teacher in our "example" is in a high school and non-tenured, she/he is observed for *one* of those 900 hours. If the teacher is tenured, the odds are two-to-one she/he will not be observed *at all*; or once in 2,700 hours!

Now I ask you, "How much improvement of instruction can we expect if the "coach" observes his players one hour per season?"

What I'm trying to say is that we, in education,

say we worry and fret about improving instruction but, in fact, it's all yarn. As a sailor might say, "They yarn'd 'bout it but they didn't do nothin'."

Listen to the yelps! "We're professionals and, as such, we work independently." How many times have I heard that yarn? Twenty-thousand dollar a year teachers are professionals and, by definition, work best independently without supervision? You know it can't be true. Engineers, physicians, lawyers, architects are all scrutinized. They are scrutinized and their work is scrutinized. The more independent the work, the greater the scrutiny. Back in the days before my commercial pilot's license yellowed and grew old, I never heard a pilot object to "check-rides." Professionals have check-rides, are supervised, observed and coached.

But, in the business of education, the typical teacher spends hundreds upon hundreds of hours teaching without *any* coaching, supervision or "check-rides." The idea that the improvement of instruction is in fact the principal's primary concern is yarn, pure odoriferous yarn. The simple arithmetic does not support the claim.

When it comes down to improving the delivery of a service, the simplest most straightforward approach to improving the delivery is to observe the existing delivery and coach for an improved delivery. Yet, in the case of public education the existing delivery goes on and on, seldom if ever observed and coached for improvement. The surest and quickest way to improve public instruction is to improve the instructing. We have to make observing and coaching attractive to the bureaucracy so that it *will* occur, regularly and in large doses.

How? How do we insert a process into the bureaucratic routine which does not threaten the oxygen supply but actually enhances it; or, has sufficient opportunity for reward that the bureaucrats are motivated to adjust to it favorably. Not being an original thinker, I steal from other, more inventive people. This time I steal from the law profession mostly and suggest we buy the observation/coaching time.

The "client" in this relationship is the teacher. The "lawyer" is the observer, or coach. Let's give the teacher five "chits," each worth 1 hour of observation time and valued at 50 dollars/hour/chit. (Don't choke yet, you'll see in a minute that the idea is not costly.) Let's also give the teacher a catalog or "yellow pages" listing of competent and approved "coaches to whom the district will pay 50 dollars for every hour which the teacher certifies (by "chit") has been devoted to observation/coaching of her/his classroom instruction.

The school district controls entry into the catalog. The "bar" exam, so to speak, is a university program on observational skills which finishes with a competency test. If the prospective coach/observer passes the rigorous competency test (and has state supervisory credentials, for legal reasons), then the prospective coach/observer is listed in the catalog with perhaps a resume.

The teacher selects from the "yellow pages" that coach he/she wants as his/her observer and makes the call and the arrangements directly. When the observation and coaching are completed, the teacher signs-off one of his/her chits and sends it into the bureaucracy. For payment, $50. The "chit" can easily be made to contain an evaluation by the teacher of the quality of service received from the coach. If the coach accumulates enough poor evaluations, he/she is dropped from the catalog.

The catalog of competent observers would soon include all principals. A crafty principal would be a damn fool not to get into the catalog as soon as possible. No hourly payment to a principal for the hours of required observation of subordinates for the purposes of employment decisions of course, that system would go on undisturbed. Payment of 50 dollars an hour would be for hours above and beyond the evaluations required by the principal's contract with the district.

Other teachers with supervisory credentials would soon want onto the list as well. Other administrators would also be eligible for the "yellow pages." It would not take long, perhaps two summers of university competency courses, before enough qualified coaches/observers would be available for teachers.

Five hours of classroom observation for every teacher, each year, would be nearly five-times as much observation/coaching of the delivery of instruction as exists now.

For a district of 2,000 teachers, i.e. something on the order of 40,000 students, we're talking about a program cost of a half-million dollars. Five times as much classroom observation for a half-million dollars, is it a good buy? I'd say so. Two thousand teachers costs about 40 million dollars a year in salaries. A half-million dollars to improve quality control by a factor of five is good business.

All the motivation for the teacher would not be altruism and carrots. Let's be straightforward about that. A teacher who doesn't use his/her five observation chits has created admissible evidence of an unwillingness or disinterest in improving his/her instruction. On the other hand, the contents of an observation, good or bad, would be protected, much as the lawyer-client relationship is protected.

Nothing, I would submit, motivates bureaucrats like the chance to make an individual buck. In education, especially, salaries are pegged to guides, ladders, ranges, etc. No matter how much better one does a job than others doing the same or similar jobs, the individual's income does not improve. In this scheme, however, one could make substantial "extra" money. For this kind of an opportunity, even a school district bureaucracy would adjust. There would be very little reason for obfuscation. The principal who is clearly a sought-after coach makes individual money and enhances his/her bureaucratic position. And most importantly the attention, the focus, shifts to instruction; the coaching and improvement of instruction.

Harry would be pleased.

"Observation" is more than sitting in the back room watching, much more. Observation, when done properly, is coaching; pure and simple coaching. When a coach works with a player, the coach first determines what it is the player is trying to do; a particular football technique is a good example. (Chosen as an example by an old coach. Former coach is more accurate. Former and old is precise.) The coach then watches the player execute the technique to identify how it could be done better. It may be a matter of timing, or footwork, or follow through, etc. Then the coach points out to the player how he/she presently is executing the technique and how to improve. The player then tries the suggested changes and practices the improved technique. The cycle of execution, observation, discussion and practice is repeated and repeated until the improvement becomes so ingrained it is practically second nature to the player. A good coach then points out to the player how he, the player, can recognize for himself any regression or departure from the improved technique. This gives the player a way to check his/her performance on his own, without the coach constantly reminding.

Much the same sort of pattern can exist for teaching. The teacher and the observer/coach can meet before the actual instruction time so the teacher can explain what it is he/she will be trying to do, a particular teaching technique or classroom management plan, for example. The coach then watches the teacher execute the technique during the instruction time. A good coach will actually take notes and develop data that can be used with the teacher after the instruction time which will help the teacher understand how he/she presently is executing the technique. The coach then identifies how it could be done better. It may be a matter of timing, habit, questioning technique, etc. The good coach points out how the teacher can recognize for him/herself any regression or departure from the improved technique in subsequent instruction. The teacher repeats and practices the new and/or improved technique until it becomes second nature.

In my first year of teaching I had an algebra class which seemed to me to be slower in understanding algebra equations than should have been the case. I asked, with much trepidation, another math teacher to come in and observe my teaching. It didn't take long for that teacher to see the problem, or one of the problems. My colleague pointed out to me after class the habit I had fallen into of writing each new equation on the blackboard from left to right. I was right handed. Each time I wrote an equation my 6'4" hulk was, in effect, covering from the students' view what I had just written as I wrote the next step in the equations solution. Of course the students were slow in answering questions I posed to them about the equation. The students hadn't seen the equation until I walked away from it and asked about it. How could they possibly have followed me through my brilliant and witty solution and understood it enough to answer my questions about it . . . they hadn't been able to see what I was doing!

"A simple little habit I should have caught myself," you say. You're probably right, but I hadn't seen it. My coach saw it and I changed my technique. My students began to show almost immediate improvement.

Just to finish the story, one of the things I did to improve was teach myself to write algebra left handed so my hulk was not in front of the equation. It took me hours and hours of practice after school but I learned. To this day I still delight in dazzling groups when I speak in a classroom by writing with either hand. Only problem is it diverts attention from what I've written to how I'm writing it. But, I'm not doing anything nearly as important at the blackboard now as I was then, so I can indulge myself.

I can remember the story of the baseball coach working with Duke Snider of the Brooklyn Dodgers, a great hitter. The coach pointed out to Snider that he had a habit of "taking" the first pitch when batting lefthanded. Opposing pitchers had caught on and Duke was finding himself one strike in the hole from the start. "The Duke" changed his habit and his production of hits rose once again.

"A little thing he should have caught himself," we might say. Probably correct, but it took a coach's observant eyes. You can be sure the baseball batting coach got more than 50 dollars an hour.

To improve instruction in our schools we've got to get in there and improve instruction. Five hours of observing/coaching may not be enough but it sure beats zero or one hour. Yarnin' about improving instruction won't get it done. Passing another law requiring more observation will only get us another law. We've got to make observing/coaching important enough to everybody involved that they will *want* to get it done. Let's buy the coach's time just as we buy their lawyer's time.

IV

DISCIPLINARIANS DO IT
WITH A SMILE

Back in the years of college "disturbances," there existed a California state college with a president by the name of S.I. Hayakawa. The so-called college "students" of other schools in the vicinity had all but paralyzed instruction in the larger, more visible universities and turned to the smaller California state facility over which S.I. Hayakawa presided.

The "students" had been successful, even beyond their wildest dreams, in bringing to heel major universities. Almost all post-secondary instruction had ceased to exist at that time in California. No one over 30 was trusted, as the "warcry" was phrased. One state college continued, providing the service for which it was created: instruction. The "students" couldn't have that.

It was only a state college and it surely continued on its assigned way merely because it had been overlooked by the "students" in the rush to bring down the larger, more prestigious universities. With all the others heeling, it was thought a casual afternoon would be all that was needed to wrap up

43

this state college. And, to assure full press coverage, the "students" announced the afternoon they had selected to take over San Francisco State College.

One detail got overlooked by the "students," one minor item. It's understandable how the oversight could occur, no other college or university president had been a problem, each had capitulated early; in melifluous tones of course. Why should the "students" have expected otherwise from a two-bit small state college president.

But, "the last college president west of the Atlantic," as we came later to call him, had other ideas. President S. I. Hayakawa spoke publicly to students, police, citizens and media, in advance. His institution had only one purpose, to provide instruction. Anyone disturbing the instruction was to be removed from campus, using as much force as needed to get the job done; "Only do it with a smile."

The appointed afternoon arrived. The confrontation materialized, the disrupters were removed, everybody smiled and instruction at San Francisco State College continued. Student disrupters were "slain by little David wearing a beret," and never recovered. Post-secondary education resumed. College president Hayakawa went on to become Senator Hayakawa.

There are three purposes for which the citizen

pays school taxes: INSTRUCTION, INSTRUC-
TION AND INSTRUCTION.

"You must understand," I am lectured, "the
student is only acting out his/her frustration with
failure."

"Yarn!" I answer.

"The minority student is striking back at the
society which oppresses him/her," I'm lectured.

"More Yarn," I answer.

"In the only way he knows how," I'm lectured.

"Yarn," I reply.

"The majority student is being pushed around,"
I'm lectured.

"Yarn," I reply.

The only reason we in public education are
allowed to reach into the public's pocket is for
instruction. The only reason a youngster is provided with public schooling, regardless of ability to
pay is instruction. Anyone, citizen, student or
staff, disturbing the instruction must be removed,
using as much force as needed to get the job done.
Only do it with a smile.

Sounds simple enough, doesn't it? Then why
doesn't it happen?

"Because it's not simple," I reply.

Some years ago I was visiting a high school and
saw a fight break out in the hallway between two
students, one white and one black. The young,
healthy looking male teacher in the room nearby

did nothing. He continued about his business, straining not to let on he heard or saw the rumpus. An assistant principal happened upon the event and broke it up. He, the assistant principal, strained not to let on he had seen the teacher straining not to let on.

Later, in the principal's office, I related what I had seen and asked the principal, "Why?" First the principal assured me what I had seen was *not* unusual teacher behavior. The particular teacher I had watched straining not to become involved had been around longer than I had judged. The teacher knew that both of the fighting students, had he stepped in to break up the fight, would have had attorneys on the scene no later than the next morning.

The white student's attorney would be suing the teacher, the principal, the superintendent and the board members collectively and individually for damages his client had incurred by the exercise of cruel and excessive restraining force used upon his client. The black student's attorney would be suing the same people for the same reasons on behalf of his client, plus he'd also be suing for a violation of his client's civil rights. Both attorneys would have in hand signed affidavits from physicians attesting to the extensive and irreparable harm the patient's psyche had incurred from the force used by the teacher. "The administration is represented by the board but the teacher would need his own lawyer and he can't afford that.''

I was young at the time and, of course, didn't believe the principal. Now that I'm older I can tell you the principal was not entirely correct. He should have added that had the genders of the students and the teacher not been the same, the teacher would have been sued for sexual abuse as well as all the other counts. And, I can tell you, had the students been young elementary school children, the charges would probably have included child abuse. Had that principal to whom I was talking that day, years ago, included the charges I've mentioned, he would have been entirely correct.

Call it a sign of the times, call it exercising one's rights, call it what you will. Conditions exist now which prompt a challenge practically every time authority is exercised. Maybe, in moderation, the challenges are helpful, deterring excessive use or abuse of authority. In the case of the teacher's role, however, the authority contained therein is fragile at best.

We all want better discipline, we say. We all want the teachers to ''crack-down'' on disruptive behavior, we say. We are all yarnin' the teacher or other school employees unless we are willing to pay for the legal costs of enforcing discipline.

If we want discipline in our schools, then item number one is a locked-up-tight, legally certain

47

assurance to every school employee that he/she will be "covered" against any claim or lawsuit resulting from the employee's execution of his/her responsibility to maintain discipline. Even if a case is found to have merit because the employee errored in, or omitted something from, his/her otherwise perfectly proper execution of the responsibility and damages are levied; even then there has to exist an assurance that the school district will pay the damages for the teacher or other employees.

You recognize the legal matter I'm raising. You recall, I'm sure, the "Good Samaritan" law for doctors. There was a short time not too many years ago when physicians were passing accidents and injuries by rather than get involved because of the lawsuits and damages being assessed against doctors who did become involved. The situation existed for only a short time because laws were enacted quickly which protected the "Good Samaritan" physician from damage if he/she became involved.

What's needed are "Good Disciplinarian" laws to go along with the "Good Samaritan" laws. That is, if we really mean what we say when we say we want good discipline; if we're not yarn'n that is.

Item number two which has to exist if we want an undisturbed instructional setting, i.e., "Discipline," are consequences for parents. In the good old days (to which I'm not advocating we return but from which I do think we can learn) a son or daughter's behavior had consequences for the parents and the rest of the family. In a stable town or settled neighborhood where people knew each other across generations, the family "name" was of substantial importance. A "good" name meant a difference at the bank, the grocery store, in the job market and at church. If you came from a "good" family and sought a job, you had a far better chance of getting one than did your competitor who did not have a family name that meant honesty, reliability and dependability. A son or daughter's misbehavior at school had a family consequence, a serious, important impact on the family name. Other societies and nations have us here. In most of our competitor nations, a child's misbehavior still seems to have consequences for the parents.

A parental consequence for the child's school behavior is all but gone from modern society. I'm not going to describe its departure nor lament its passing, I'm merely going to posit that it's gone. What I want us to think about is school discipline in the absence of parental consequences.

Telephone the parent these days about a misbehaving child and the parent (or guardian) is likely to react to the call not as one on the verge of suffering in the market place or the neighborhood. The parent or guardian reacts more like the child's attorney. "Oh yes, I've been expecting your call. My child told me about this incident and he/she says . . ." The parent assumes the role of the attorney defending the child, or worse a "judge" deciding whether what the child said is right or what the school official is saying is right! The concept that the school teachers and officials, along with the parent are, together, trying to develop a self-controlling adult is gone.

Each year the Gallup Polster organization conducts a scientific survey of adults across the nation on behalf of an educational magazine, *Phi Delta Kappan*. Each year the same question is asked, "What do you see as the major problem in school(s)?" Each year the same answer heads the list: "Discipline." I have yet to read of any follow-up questions, even the simple question, "Why?" The implication in the question and in the answer at present seems to me quite clear. School teachers and officials are viewed as solely responsible for discipline. The idea that an offspring's behavior has consequences for the parent seems to have all but disappeared. We somehow have to restore it.

We have to restore parental consequences for a child's behavior, but we have to do it in modern terms. Lamenting the loss of family tightness, small community structure and neighborhood meaning is pure yarn if that's all we do. We can't just sit around and lament the loss of the "good old days," while other nations pass us by. We can't just yarn about it.

Let's start with the almighty modern dollar. Let's require that the employer, the parent's employer, be notified by phone during the regular work hours every time one of his employee's children distrupts the school's instructional setting. Let's require the employer to send the parent, without pay, to the school immediately. The employer is not going to like that kind of work-scene disruption and the employed parent will learn very quickly that his/her child's behavior has a parental consequence.

In the case of the driver's licenses, the child's driver's license: let's automatically suspend driver's licenses for disruptive behavior. Insurance statistics point out time and again that achieving students are safer drivers. Let's get the disruptive student off the road and into the parent's care (and car).

In the matter of damage to school property, let's make it an automatic requirement that the parent's wages or income be "garnished" until repayment is complete. Automatic deductions from the pay-check, unemployment check, stock dividend check, tax-return, *et al.* will be required until restitution is complete.

These kinds of consequences may seem harsh but they fall far short of the kinds of consequences which used to derive from living in a stable town or settled neighborhood where people knew each other across generations. The kinds of things I have suggested last only as long as the disruptive behavior lasts, in the old tight-family setting consequences could and did last lifetimes.

Item one, assure the teacher or other school official against legal entanglements when he/she acts to maintain discipline, much as we assure the "Good Samaritan" physician. Item two, restore parental consequences for a child's behavior. Restore it in modern terms, right smack in the pocketbook.

Maybe I ought to define the words I keep using, "disruptive behavior." It's important that this term be defined before going on to item three. The focus in school is on instruction, should be on instruction; has to be on INSTRUCTION, INSTRUCTION and INSTRUCTION. Any action by any person which distracts a learner's attention from the instruction going on is disruptive behavior by the person causing the distraction.

Item three which has to exist if we want an undisturbed instructional setting; i.e., discipline, is a focus *on* the instructional setting; *not* a focus on the disrupter. Schools are judicially sensitive and follow the present-day judicial mind-set which focuses upon the criminal at the expense of the victim. A child who comes to school intending to learn, who pays attention and behaves, but who can't learn because the instructional setting is disrupted by another, that well-behaving young. .r is a victim.

Let me see if I can explain what I mean by focusing on the instructional setting, not the disrupter, with a small example. Take a simple thing like coming late to class. Thirty kids in the class, 29 hard at work, one enters the classroom late. When that late entry occurs 29 students and one instructor are going to be distracted. If we keep the focus on the instructional setting, then we have to conclude that late entry is disruptive and should not occur. We'd have to say, "If you are late for class you don't get in; report to the principal. (Period) The instructional setting must not be disrupted.

If we let our focus wander, we begin to think about the poor kid who was late because he stopped to help a little old lady cross the street and how that poor innocent kid will miss his class. The late entering student will, if allowed in, disrupt the 29 kids and teacher who made it to class on time. We cannot let that happen. We must keep our focus on the instructional setting, not on the disrupter.

If we can see in this small example how the instructional setting must be the focus, the heavier disrupters come easily into perspective. Our two fighters in the earlier examples are disrupting the normal progress of the others in the building to/from classes. Both fighters have to be removed from the school setting. With a focus on the instructional setting, questions about who started the fight, who was defending what great universal truth, etc. all become moot. Both of them disrupted the school setting, therefore, out.

Our fourth item, if we are to have discipline, is largely an internal bureaucracy when it comes to accomplishing it but a general item for us all to understand. If we preserve our focus upon the instructional setting and remove the disrupters from the setting, we will soon have ourselves a goodly supply of disrupters out of the regular schools. What to do with them?

Our fourth item: Treat the disruptive (with a smile upon the face, of course) as disruptive; and keep treating the disruptive as disruptive until he/she proves otherwise by modified behavior. Nobody should be returned to the regular instructional setting on the basis of a promise he/she won't do it again. If discipline is to exist, it's not the school officials who have to prove the disruptive youngster should be out, it's the kid who has to prove he/she should be back in. Nobody should be returned to the regular school setting after serving a "sentence."

We do the latter bit all the time in schools and it's ineffective. It does not modify nor prevent disruptive behavior, it rewards it in a "red badge of courage" way. How many times have we seen a principal publish a "list of offenses and punishments"? We even credit such a publication as a sign of a get-rough principal. All it really does is identify some behaviors for kids who hadn't thought of them yet and motivate others to find other disruptive behaviors not on the list; and, everybody focuses on the offender and the offenses. We don't run prisons and a principal's job is not as easy as a warden's. A principal doesn't (or shouldn't) mete out punishments, she/he teaches acceptable behavior. "Disrupt the instructional setting and you're out," ought to replace lists. ". . . and you don't return until you have modified your behavior," ought to be made very clear to everyone from day one.

"If we do as you suggest, we will have more kids out of school than in!" I can hear the response to what I've written. First, if we did (have hordes of disrupters), we would simply have a clear indication of the enormity of the task facing the teaching institution; the numbers of children still in need of learning how to control and discipline themselves; and the instructional setting for those kids who are not out would be secure.

Second, if the numbers of disrupters were large at the outset, the numbers would decline rapidly. Most youngsters do know self-control and will behave acceptably if they know what's expected of

them and know the consequence of behaving un-
acceptably. As a matter of fact, we might begin to
see principals publishing lists of "acceptable
behavior," i.e., focusing upon the instructional
setting.

Third, the actual numbers of disrupters would
stabilize at perhaps five percent of the total student
population. Six thousand secondary students
would yield something in the neighborhood of
three hundred serious disrupters (I'm not talking
about the criminal element, we'll come to that
later.) And, the remaining 95 percent would have a
stable and secure instructional setting.

What to do with the five percent? First, we
protect them from judicial intervention. Yes, we
protect them from the courts. We do that by
treating each and every one as an individual about
whom we have great concern. In other words, we
keep the disrupter's attorney from running to the
court to get the kid reinstated into the regular
school setting because his client is supposedly being
persecuted. Unless we do this the kid is back in the
regular setting before she/he has learned how to
modify the disruptive behavior. Hence, we begin by
exhibiting great concern, understanding and em-
pathy for the disrupting individual. And, we do it
all with a smile.

We spend days testing the youngster. (Days
which, of course, keep the disruptive out of the

regular school and regular instructional setting.) Psychological tests, interest inventories, achievement tests, you name it. We introduce the individual to the school district's discipline officer, hopefully an attorney or para-attorney, who explains to the individual his/her rights, advises that he/she can retain an attorney, offers to have the school district obtain and pay for one if the youngster and family can't. It is explained to the individual that she/he is not to return to regular school property for any reason under penalty of arrest for trespassing . . . because this youngster is now assigned to the district's "alternative school" until such time as his/her behavior has changed to what is acceptable.

And what's the district's alternative school? It's that public school in which is provided, from the view of the youngster, the minimum education required of the public by state law. (Remember, there is no federal Constitutional statement about education; it's one of those matters "reserved" to the states.) The youngster sees a remote, delapidated, old school building in which half the lights work, one third of the radiators and none of the airconditioners. He/she is transported there on school buses with square wheels and broken springs. The faculty looks like under-cover agents for the narcotics squad and the school runs year round. There's n football, no band, no clubs, no lawn. In short, the youngster and his parent are presented with a scene which makes the statement, "This is the minimum the public must, by law, provide you; the rest (bands, clubs, lawns, air-conditioning, athletics, et al.) the public provides to those who are interested in instruction and who demonstrate their interest with regular, daily, acceptable behavior."

The narc-looking teacher (with a smile on his scraggly face of course) greets the youngster and her/his parent, and probably attorney, with copies of the five most recent court decisions upholding the alternative school's operation and a behavioral contract which both the parent and youngster must sign. The behavioral contract spells it all out. In sum it says, "This is the last school year you may ever attend at the public's expense unless you modify your behavior. Satisfy us you've shaped-up and we'll consider recommending your return to the regular school in which you were disruptive, but spit out of turn here and you are out."

I concede. It will take money to build and operate a "good" alternative school. The faculty must be expert at modifying adolescent behavior as well as having expertise in the academics and special education. The year round operation of the school provides an avenue through which extra pay can be paid these teachers. The student-teacher ratio has to be half the regular school ratio so that the youngster gets twice the attention. The building(s) have to look like the last resort. It's not inexpensive to operate a well-camouflaged instructional setting in which the hidden curriculum is behavior modification, but the money will be well spent if it assures a safe and stable regular school instructional setting.

In years past there were schools for the disruptive student and many argue such schools were abandoned because they didn't work. My idea of what needs to happen, if we are serious about discipline, obviously draws upon history but with one critical difference. In the alternative school I've described the youngster can "escape" back to the regular school by modifying his/her behavior. The disruptive youngster is not "sentenced" to the alternative school for a fixed length of time during which he/she need do nothing but "put in time." Nor is he/she sentenced there permanently, no matter what.

The disruptive student who alleges his/her behavior has changed and can prove it to the satisfaction of the regular school principal and faculty with supporting testimony, is returned to the regular instructional setting. The formerly disruptive student's testimony, her/his parent's testimony, the minister's testimony, the employer's testimony (if she/he has a part time job) and alternative school faculty testimony would all be necessary to convince the regular school principal and faculty to readmit the youngster: on one condition, he/she must report his/her new progress regularly to each person who "stood-up" for the youngster. In this fashion we create a support group for the youngster. Through ceremony we say what we mean, "Acceptable behavior is important stuff, in school and beyond: and we are not yarn'n you kid."

One last item, then I shall step down from my soap box. It's an item which can do, is doing, more damage to American public education than any other single factor. Even in the middle of the Atlantic, a thousand miles away, I still found myself becoming emotional about it.

The item is crime. Somehow there has developed in our society a confusion between the word "crime" and the word "discipline." If we really want effective American public education, we must sort out the confusion between these two words.

Ours is the only society on the planet where a person who has committed a crime is deliberately sent in among the young and most impressionable segment of our population. You don't think we do that? We do it everyday, all across the nation.

Any criminal who is a juvenile is returned to school!

No other society on the face of this earth, now or through history, has ever sent criminals to live and function among its young in the public schools and then bemoaned the "loss of discipline" among their young in those schools. We are guilty of the biggest bale of woolen yarn imaginable.

Simply stated, there is no way a society can have discipline in its public schools as long as that society deliberately sentences the most impressionable and innocent to live and work with criminals. Our society, so dependent on a respect for "law," sentences its young to learn among the very people who have demonstrated no respect for the "law."

My definition of a criminal may be at odds with the accepted definition. I'm defining a criminal as anyone who has committed a crime. (Drugs, robbery, theft, rape, assault, murder, etc.) The definition within which we require our public school teachers and officials to operate is different. The operating definition of a "criminal" for the public schools is anyone who has committed a crime and is not a juvenile.

As things stand presently, two high school seniors could sell drugs downtown and get arrested. One could be prosecuted because he/she is 19 , the other returned to school because he/she is 17! The net result of the present law(s) would return the drug pusher in among his prospects. Who is learning what about the law?

I don't want to be an alarmist but consider this

drug example from the viewpoint of the adult drug pusher. The juvenile is the desired salesperson! The adult pusher will employ the juvenile because of the protection the present law(s) provide his/her drug operation.

I have talked to junior high school principals who've told me of children in their respective schools with high-paying after-school jobs as "juveniles" (10-12-14 years old). These kids are paid to run drugs, shoplift, steal cars, you name it, by adult criminals who play on the law's naivete.

This is a true story. I know of a superintendent in whose district two seniors were arrested for rape. One senior was prosecuted, he was 18. The other senior was returned to school, he was 17 and a juvenile. The superintendent did a little homework and found the 16-year-old granddaughter of the judge in one of the high schools. He arranged for this six foot juvenile to be assigned to the same high school as the granddaughter, and as luck would have it, the hall locker next to the granddaughter's was unassigned. Within a week the judge had decided to prosecute both offenders as adults. The "juvenile" was arrested and incarcerated without bail pending trial.

Unfortunately, there aren't enough judges' and legislators' relatives in the public schools to treat with the problem as that superintendent did. We must change the law.

We must remove from school the student who would otherwise be convicted as a felon except for his/her age. Our primary objective remains INSTRUCTION, INSTRUCTION, INSTRUCTION.

In every state, I believe it's every state, a felony conviction for a teacher removes his/her license to teach. We've said, clearly, we do not want felons in our schools; unless the felon is a juvenile. Our laws about juveniles need changing. If we aren't yarnin' about discipline, we must clear up the confusion and not mix the juvenile criminals with the juvenile students.

What to do with the juvenile criminal? Let's sneak up on the answer. We know where we don't want the juvenile criminal. We don't want him/her in among the adult criminals learning more crime and we don't want him/her in among the juvenile students teaching crime. This juvenile criminal is the one person we must extricate from the regular public school (and the home setting) to a full-time boarding-school situation.

Expensive, I'll agree, but, what's the alternative?

In sum, if we are serious about "good" discipline in our schools, then there are some items we must do; now. We must (1) legislate "Good Samaritan" type laws protecting the teacher, (2) legislate consequences for parents if they don't parent, (3) focus on preserving the fragile instructional setting against disruption, (4) modify the disrupter's behavior, and (5) legislate criminal juveniles out of the instructional setting. These things must happen if, and only if, we intend to cut the yarn about our desire for discipline in our schools.

V

UNIONS
(Everybody Plays Ball)

Over the course of time man has been operating on this planet some really great documents have been written. The Magna Carta comes to mind quickly. It is one of the early, if not the first, document(s) in which is written the idea that the sovereign king's subjects have some "rights." A very recent really great document is the United States Constitution. It is one of the few, if not the only, document(s) in which is written the idea of "the balance of power."

Three branches of government (Judicial, Executive, Legislative; remember that class in school?). No one of the branches has enough power to work independently. No one branch can abuse what power it has for long before one, or both, of the other branches step in to check the abuse and restore balance ("checks and balances" was the title my teacher used.)

What an ingenious concept, the balance of power. It allows for new ideas to become law, but only after the idea has run the gauntlet of the independent "branches" of the whole. The authors of our Constitution deliberately wrote a document for an unfinished government, expecting us to improve things as we learned, but assuring that our ideas for change first pass muster.

We can see this same "balance of power" concept in subsequent local governing bodies in our country, even in the governing bodies of the local educational systems. The names may differ, school committees in some states, trustees in others, boards of education in most, but the "balance" concept seems to run through all the local laws creating and providing for the governance of the free public school. The judicial arm of the local balance is generally reserved to the state's courts and not usually realized to be the judicial branch of the educational governance plan which it is. The legislative branch is the board of education and the executive is the school superintendent. The board has extensive powers, the superintendent has extensive powers, but neither can get much done without the other. And, if/when the board and the executive conspire to abuse the powers, the judicial steps in.

State laws creating public education are written for an unfinished public school system, expecting us to improve upon the initial construction as we learned, but assuring that ideas for improvement and change first pass muster. An ingenious concept; frustrating, at times, for the executive and frustrating, at times, for the board, but improvements on the initial construction have happened, with minimal subsequent regression.

The initial "grammar schools" idea was built into the kindergarten through high school, in some places through junior college, universal public education we have now; proof that change and improvement to schools has happened in the past. By the end of World War II we had an educational system worthy of being copied by other nations.

"Why then," I asked myself as I bobbed along in my little boat on the ocean, "Why then, won't it change now?"

It's still the same system of checks and balances, a judicial branch responsible to the citizens either by direct election or by appointment at the hands of someone directly elected by the citizens, a legislative branch where the board members are elected directly or appointed by someone directly elected by the citizens and an executive branch where the superintendent is elected, either directly or indirectly. Why won't it respond to the citizens' demands for change nowadays, even when the citizens are willing to increase funding for "anything but more of the same?"

I threw the answer overboard three or four times before I finally let it come aboard and stay for inspection. Is it possible that the balance, the three branches concept is yarn nowadays? Finally, I allowed the heresy aboard in order to inspect it.

Are the three branches, the balance of power situation through which change could and did occur, now yarn? Are there four branches to educational governance nowadays? Has a fourth branch grown since World War II? There is still the judicial branch, its powers are no different. There is still the legislative, or board of education, branch. There is still the executive, or superintendent branch, but is there now a fourth branch: the *union* branch? Change came about in the past, albeit slowly, but now change has virtually stopped since WW II. Has unionism tipped the balance from conservative change to preservation?

Unionism around our house was a revered word when I was growing up. Relatives in the steel mills of Baltimore were better off because of their unions. Wages were higher, benefits were improving and safety in the mill was much better, all because of the unions.

The concept of unions in the private sector has certainly proven to be sound. The employees organized and their representatives negotiated directly with the owners' representatives over wages, hours and conditions of employment. Compromise brought agreement. When compromise reached an impasse and the workers withheld services, i.e. went on strike, the contest of pocketbook damage was joined. Whose pocketbook would collapse first, the owners' because they weren't making any money or the workers because they had no wages? The financial strain brought both parties back to reason.

The government's role was to maintain a balance of power between owners and workers (there's that concept again). The National Labor Relations Board was the legislative creation that held the day-to-day balance and kept the owners and workers at the bargaining table. The process has gotten quite complicated, true, but it still works pretty well. When the process seems to have forsaken all reason, the forces in the private sector market place bring everybody back to their senses.

I seem to recall that the private sector concept of unionism began moving heavily into the public sector back in the late 1950's and 1960's. I can remember pouring over government statistics on per-capita income back then to see if they held any clue to the reason(s) for the movement. I can recall graphing the per capita income in New Jersey over the years for which the statistics were supplied.

From about 1950 to 1970 the per-capita income was on a gentle but steady rise. In general, things looked good for everybody working in business. Then I added another line to the graph. I added the "per-teacher" income for the same years. The two lines were essentially parallel up to about 1960. It seemed to me I was looking at a picture of the "pecking-order" position of teachers relative to the economy. The pecking-order for teachers through the 1950's held constant for everybody in the private sector.

Then something happened around 1960. The per-teacher income curve no longer paralleled the per-capita curve. Teachers were falling behind. They were dropping down in the economic pecking order. The displacement of the teacher downwardly in the economic pecking order coincided with the rise in public-sector unionizing. Unionism was helping the private sector worker so, quite understandably, teachers lifted the whole concept right over into the public-sector.

Did it work? On my little graph it seemed to have worked. Five years after unionism in New Jersey the curves had resumed their relative marching positions across my page. Unionism had restored the economic pecking order of the public-sector teachers relative to the private sector workers.

A story slightly to the side. I should have thrown that graph in the trashcan. Instead I started talking about it. I argued to the New Jersey State Teachers Union Leadership (Association, I think they called themselves) that the union movement had not really improved the teachers position, merely restored it to what it had been for decades before. Not a small accomplishment by any standard but not the "victory" union leaders were proclaiming. As a result I got tagged as anti-union, me of all people. I should have kept my mouth shut. (Probably ought to be keeping my mouth shut now, too.)

We're into the late 80's. What about the effect of unions now that they've been around in most of public education for nearly a quarter of a century? Well, I argue that the economic pecking order for teachers has not improved. Teachers are not better off now relative, say to engineers for example, than they were twenty-five years ago.

Teachers might not be as bad off as they might have been in the pecking order of things had there not been the unionism movement, but the idea that teachers are better off economically is yarn. Unions certainly turned things around in the early 70's and kept the bottom from falling out, but they don't seem to me to have done for the public sector worker all that they did for the private sector worker. Using the popular language of the day, unions are a good safety-net institution. Are they important? Yes. Are they change-agents? No. Five times out of six, bargaining results in preservation; not change.

Let's look at bargaining. Two parties at the table, the union and the board. After 15 plus years of this I am convinced there are three phases involved. The first phase I call the "B/M phase," short for Benevolence/Malevolence phase. The board is heard to say, "After all these years we've

71

worked so hard for you teachers, this is the way you thank us?'' The union is heard to say, ''After all these years of putting up with such terrible conditions, this is the way you thank us?''

The second phase I call the ''adversary phase.'' When one or both of the parties at the table are in this mental phase we hear one or the other claim to have ''won.'' ''We won a ten-percent raise,'' or ''We beat off an attempt to get major medical coverage.''

The third phase I call the ''same-boat phase.'' When one of the parties at the bargaining table is in this mental phase we hear very little except perhaps, ''We're working to clear up our differences.'' When both parties are in the same-boat phase, each party to the bargaining realizes that both parties are in the same boat and, if one end of the boat goes down, both ends go down. There are no winners or losers, just survivors. If the boat is going to get anywhere, everybody in the boat is going to have to work together.

What we have in the bargaining situation is a ''two by three matrix,'' two independent parties each of whom can be in any one of three phases at any time. What are the chances that both parties will be in the same-boat phase at the same time so that bargaining can make real headway? The chances are one in six. In other words, the chances of getting real educational improvement from the bargaining table are about the same chances as shooting crap. Five times out of six, somebody's going to be foot-dragging and bargaining will result in preservation; not change.

The idea that unionism brings real institutional change in the public sector, especially in public education, is (unfortunately) yarn.

If the odds were against unionism resulting in institutional change in public education, the odds were in favor of unionism resulting in political change. It's in the political arena that the preservation ethos of public sector unionism has had its greatest impact, far greater than in the private sector.

If you were the head of a local union and sat down across the bargaining table from an especially obstreperous board member, how long would it take you to realize that the best way to deal with the board member was to vote him out of office? Local board elections traditionally bring out a minimum of voters. You're sitting there at the table representing a well organized, well educated, active and astute constituency who, if voting as a bullet, could bring down the obstreperous board member. It wouldn't take you very long to see that the simplest way to get what you want from the bargaining table is to control the other side of the table. You would, no doubt, see clearly that the strike is not the public-sector union's most persuasive weapon, the

73

vote is the most powerful weapon.

This political factor is something that was not brought along in the transfer of private sector unionism to the public sector. It's something entirely unique to the public sector. In private sector bargaining the company owner is the company owner. When he's sitting at the negotiating table he's not facing people on the other side who can take away his/her ownership. In the private sector the two sides are even and independent. The owner's the owner, the union's the union.

An elected board member, sitting down at a negotiating table, sees something altogether different when he/she looks across the table. The board member sees the largest single voting block in the next election glaring back at him. The two sides are not even. The union owns, or will very shortly own, both sides of the table.

Not only has the balance of power at the bargaining table changed, the balance of power where boards are elected has changed, and that's the majority of the boards across the country. The union-elected board member is the union's and not just at the bargaining table. The board member elected by the union is the union's when it comes time to hire/fire/elect a superintendent.

Superintendents are not usually dumb and almost always crafty. A superintendent counts votes. It's not long, not long at all, before the superintendent knows where the power lies and the superintendent is the union's: and everybody plays ball.

The original concept of checks and balances becomes yarn. The institution becomes dedicated to the preservation of the status-quo, three inches of boiler-plate surrounded by foot-thick concrete. It's a great set-up. The teacher inside the organization enjoys a level of insulation and protection from pressures to change or improve the likes of which have never before existed. And everybody plays ball.

Other interest groups, other than the teachers' union, what happens to them? They find themselves under-represented or not represented at all. Let's examine one interest group as an example. Let's examine the parents in an innercity school on the single issue of experienced "good" teachers. Inner-city schools have notoriously high teacher turnover. A promising young teacher starting out at an innercity school gets some seniority and moves out to a "good" school. The parents complain to the board. "We want stability on our school's faculty, and we want experience," they say. The answer, "There's nothing we can do, the union contract gives the teacher with seniority the right to first choice of any position for which he/she is qualified. The union contract gives the teacher the right to refuse a transfer assignment," etc., etc. . . . So the situation does not change in the innercity school even though practically every individual, when confronted with the situation, will agree "something ought to be done." And every teacher knows the school would do a better job with a "good," stable faculty.

The innercity parents in our example, where are they? They are on the outside. To them the school has demonstrated by its own action (or inaction) that it is just an extension, or an arm, of "the man"; the school is part of the "they" that has no interest in them or their kids.

I don't mean to portray anyone in my little example as uncaring, or devious, or malicious. The union did well by its members in getting them what they wanted in the contract, a seniority clause. Teachers want to teach well. They feel a greater sense of fulfillment when their students learn. "Good" students learn more, they are students who want to learn. Good teachers move to good students. No one has been malicious. But, nothing changed, no one changed, no one can change and the parents are alienated. And instruction in the school? "Who gives a damn?"

Let's take an example at a suburban school, just so none of us think the problem is not ours. First rate, high achieving, top quality high school; parents want a tutor program in the students' junior year prior to the college board exams. The parents go to the board. The answer, "There's nothing we can do, the union contract says each teacher teaches a maximum of five periods, every teacher in your school has five periods and the right to refuse a sixth. We can't afford another teacher," etc., etc. . . . So the situation does not change in the suburban school either. No one is at fault here. The union has gotten a good contract term defining teacher load so none of its members are taken advantage of. A good teacher wants to teach her/his five periods and prepare during her/his sixth and do a good job.

The suburban parents in our example, where are they? They are on the outside. To them the school has demonstrated its unresponsiveness. "Who gives a damn about my child?"

I repeat. No one is at fault, not the teachers, not the unions, not the boards, not the superintendents. It's just that we've lost that beautiful concept of the balance of power. In the presence of the balance of power, change can occur. A group who wants change can muster enough power to tip the balance and cause change.

The more concrete that gets added around the boiler plate, the more power has to be accumulated to cause change. The contest moves from the local power scene to the board of education power scene, from the board scene to the state legislature power scene (where, by the way, we are now), from the state scene to the federal power scene and, finally, somebody says, "Hell, if it takes that much power to change the schools, let's just go around them altogether." And the word "voucher" enters the power language. And free, universal, public education goes down the scupper (the drain).

I'm not yarnin' anybody. Either the schools change themselves or we lose our "lock" on the public.

Remember the railroads? There was a time when the railroads had a "lock" on the movement of passengers and cargo in this country. Owners, management, workers and unions all played ball together and the public could not get the service they wanted. What happened? The public went around the railroads.

How did the public go around the recalcitrant railroads? Somebody invented the word "interstate" and the federal government ribboned the country with concrete highways. What concrete the government didn't put down as highways they put down as runways. The railroads became dinosaurs.

Now we have the word "voucher." The public, in a free country, cannot, will not be locked into public services unresponsive to the public. Somebody will invent a way around the recalcitrant public service (and servants).

I personally have no problem with the idea of giving each parent a voucher for the tax money raised for the education of his/her child. As a matter of fact I'd love it. I know I could raise the capital, put together a damn good school, even franchise it like McDonalds, and make a good return for my investors. I could even create different menus. You want a religious school? I've got one for you. A good old-fashioned discipline school? Got one of those, too. You want the college-prep model? Sure.

I'd love it personally. I could make a bundle of money and never look back.

As long as I didn't think about Jefferson and Madison and Franklin and those guys with their noble experiment, I'd be O.K.

Unions in the public sector are an asset and a liability, more asset than liability; especially in large bureaucracies. Bureaucrats will be bureaucrats and, as such, tend to hide mistakes rather than correct them. When it comes to a mistake about an individual human being it's nice to know, as a chief executive, that there is a strong independent entity which will cry "foul" if the error is being covered up instead of rectified.

One occasion jumps immediately to mind. The leadership of the union met with me in one of our regular monthly meetings and said, "Look, we've got a member who says she filled out her application for medical coverage shortly after employment and handed it to her supervisor. Now, when she's pregnant, your personnel department tells her they have no record of her taking the medical coverage. She's young, new and scared. We've got to do something." Within two days we "found" that lady's application, made the necessary protestations to the insurance carrier that we had been at fault and her name should have appeared on the list we sent them at application time. We got her covered. We also rebuilt our procedures to assure a double-entry system of verification at application times. Maybe my personnel department was correct, maybe the lady was correct; who cares. The important thing was the union brought it to my attention. Without them I'm afraid we'd have had a "rules are rules" situation in that bureaucracy.

Nonetheless, the "balance" problem remains. That same union leader interviewed each candidate for the board and decided who would receive the union's "support." And union support meant two things, votes and money; a generous portion of each. Other local interest groups couldn't even come close to matching either.

In the 1984 elections, the National Education Association appears to have been one of the top five contributors of money to selected national candidates. It's done quite legally through their political action committee. They were right up there with the American Medical Association, National Association of Realtors and United Auto

Workers. That is power.

Again, there's nothing devious or illegal about this political activity. It's just that none of the other heavy contributors get, also, to select the company owners. The United Auto Workers do not have the opportunity also to select the board of directors of Chrysler. Recall, please, when Chrysler got itself into a sling, the company changed its ways. The UAW co-operated, I am sure, but it was co-operating with an equally independent entity, i.e. the company owners. UAW didn't interview and "support" the Chrysler board, then turn around and bargain with the board whom they had elected. The "balance"of interests was still there at that bargaining table. And, I would suggest, just as a distant observer, I'll bet both parties were in the same-boat stage.

We've got to restore the balance in the governance of American public education. Restricting public sector unionism is not an answer. We all have our constitutional right to assemble, join, contribute and vote as we please, some do it better than others.

Somehow we've got to assure that those governing school committees, trustees or boards of education, however they're titled, have within them representation of all or most of the major interest groups; no one of which is unduly dominant. The citizens against taxes, the business community, the realtors,

81

the parents, the conservatives, the liberals, et al. have to know that the governance of public education is balanced; not owned by any one interest group.

Unions are strong and dominant at the local level. Unions are strong but not dominant at the state level. Let's require that board members be appointed by the governor. For a governor to be elected he/she has to have the support of more than one interest group. A governor, of whatever political persuasion, has the balance of interest groups concept running through his/her veins like corpuscles. He/she would know, instinctively, that he/she can't risk "giving" the board to any one interest group.

Governors appoint boards and committees around the state all the time. They're tooled-up for it. They use many of the appointments as ways in which to thank various people and groups for support given, or ways to woo various groups for future support. It's the political process at work.

Members of boards of education are not paid for the work (not even expenses in most cases) so the appointment would hardly be political patronage. Member's terms can be made longer than a governor's term of office and staggered so no one governor in one term would get to appoint a majority of a board. Education is a state responsibility (although many a state politico tries to shun the responsibility because it can be extremely volatile at times). The state funds its public education (to varying degrees but more and more heavily). A state level appointee would likely have "access" into that political arena more so than a locally elected, or locally appointed individual.

I've not focused much attention upon the minority of boards whose members are locally appointed now. The appointment by a locally elected official or council can still suffer from the predominance of one powerful local interest group, albeit slightly removed. Besides, I've watched many a local city or county council with "dependent" boards take the heat for tax increases resulting strictly from additional school requirements laid on by state legislatures. Education is, constitutionally, a state function. No new problem would arise if these appointments became the governor's responsibility along with all other school boards presently elected locally.

In all cases (gubernatorial appointees) politics would still occur. Governors would listen to local officials, local interest groups, state officials, state interest groups and political parties. We ought not try to prevent the politics of school governance, just balance it.

No new bureaucracy needed, no costs involved. As a matter of fact costs might be reduced by reducing local election costs in poorly attended off-years when school board voting comes up alone. No one's particularly disenfranchised because only ten percent of the eligible voters usually turn out. And in exchange we take a positive step toward rebalancing the power distribution between what are supposed to be balanced branches of education's governance.

"Cumbersome," you say.

"Maybe," I'll reply. Let's inspect an extreme case. New Jersey has something like six-hundred school districts with nine-member boards; fifty-four hundred appointments! But, if they were six-year terms, staggered 1-2-1-2-1-2, the maximum load a governor might see in any one year would be twelve hundred or so appointments. In a four-year term the governor would make about thirty-six hundred appointments. In the best of all possible New Jerseys, maybe the governor would rely on his cabinet-level State Commissioner of Education. The situation would not be unmanageable.

Alabama has about one hundred twenty-five school districts with five member boards. With six-year terms the governor would have a maximum of one-hundred twenty-five or so appointments in any one year with one off-year. In a four-year term the governor would make about five hundred appointments.

In neither case does the magnitude of appointments represent a deterrent to the proposition. The six-year term for each board member represents stability and experience. The objective is a restoration of the balance of power and an increase in the number of interest groups represented on the local education governing boards; right down a governor's alley. Education is a state function.

With tenure, with union support, with union political action committees and with locally controlled boards of education under-representing various segments of the community into alienation, we've just about reduced public education's responsiveness down to the responsiveness level of the railroad's. Pardon the pun but, if we don't do something to get this thing back on the track, the public's going to desert us.

Thinking the public is still with us may be yarn.

VI

TIME
(Keeping The Tide In)

There's an old adage "Time and tide wait for no man." Don't believe it.

There's also the old story of the king whose court assistants convinced him he was so great that he could even command the tides. The king stood on the beach and commanded the waters to "stay." When he dried off and reflected upon what had happened, I am sure he realized that he'd just learned the hard way the lesson every chief executive officer (superintendents especially) has to learn. Subtly and most times without malice, assistants will pump the ego right on out of touch with reality. When the king in the old story had dried his head and put his towel away he probably resolved to himself to beware of ego pumpers that surround him and, when he hears them pumping, "Won't believe it."

Man can keep the tide in, however. People can succumb to the subtle influences of ego-pumping. Whole communities can lose touch with reality, even entire professions.

In Plymouth, England there is a place called

Millbay Dock. Plymouth is on the southern coast of England and the tides are regularly 18 feet. When they tied a cargo ship alongside a wharf in Plymouth with the tide in, a person unloading the ship's cargo could heft his load onto his back and walk across the deck and step off directly onto the wharf. Within about 12 hours, however, the load had to be carried from the deck 18 feet up a ladder to reach the wharf. The tide would have gone out and the cargo vessel would lower 18 feet.

Not a good way to do business. There is too much time wasted in the loading and unloading of cargo. Time, in the merchant marine business, has long meant money. Something had to be done about the situation. With an 18 foot tide, Plymouth was not as attractive a port for cargo vessels as other ports. The inventive English solved the problem centuries ago very nicely. They surrounded the water on three and a half sides with a great stone wall and put a water-proof gate in the remaining half side.

While the tide was high they opened the gate, brought in the cargo vessel and closed the gate behind it. When the tide outside the gate went out, the water in the Millbay Dock was locked in with the vessel. The deck remained level with the wharf thereafter. The vessel and the tide were kept in the lock and stayed inside while the workers unloaded.

A good solution. Not, however, the best solution

for modern times. A cargo vessel that arrived off Plymouth with only a portion of its cargo to be off-loaded at Plymouth had still to go into the bay to be unloaded and stay in there a full cycle of the tide even though it was ready to go on its way long before the gates could be opened.

English ingenuity to the rescue. A short distance up river from Millbay Dock there is a new installation. Instead of surrounding the water on all four sides, this time they built only two great walls. The two long walls are parallel to each other and far enough apart for a ship to tie up between them. Riding on top of each wall is the motorized base of a huge crane. So huge is the base that the crane actually rides back and forth above the superstructure of the cargo vessel.

The crane operator lowers his hook from above the ship down to the cargo deck and lifts the cargo high above the ship. The motorized bases move the whole thing, crane and cargo, into the shore line and the operator lowers the cargo onto the shore.

No longer is tide a factor. It makes no difference to the crane operator how far below him the ship rides. If the tide is out, he simply lets out 18 more feet of cable to get his hook to the cargo deck.

No longer is the gate a factor. If the vessel has only a portion of its cargo to be off-loaded at Plymouth, the vessel departs as soon as the cargo is lifted off and the vessel is ready.

"What, pray tell, does this have to do with education?" you ask. While sitting in my little sailboat in Millbay Dock, nervously awaiting the gates to be opened so I could get out and race across the Atlantic, it struck me the situation had a great deal to do with American public education, especially high schools.

Every September we open the gate and the "tide" carries in a new ninth grade class. We close the gate behind these 14 year-olds and lock them in for four years. They don't get out 'til we reopen the gate four years later. Some may be ready to go out after two years, but they must stay. Others may be ready to go after two and a half years, but they must stay. Everyone must stay four years, until the gate is opened for them and we say they may go.

True, there are a few who get out early, but it's generally forever thereafter to their detriment. Some few manage to flunk out, some few make such a disruption they're thrown out. But, in order to get out without having some sort of a stigma attached for life, one must wait four years until the gates are reopened.

If you try and tell me that every 14 year-old, needs to be locked into high school for the subsequent four years; and, after exactly four years, that every one of those 17 year-olds is ready to go, I am going to tell you that you are yarnin' me. There is no way that all 14 year-olds were created so similarly that every last one of them must spend years 14, 15, 16 and 17 in high school and then all, at the same miraculous date in June, are ready to go to sea! That's yarn.

There's a movement afloat in many states called "basic competencies." It's a very admirable attempt to assure that every youngster who graduates from high school has the basic competencies needed to function in the adult world. It's a long overdue effort to "raise standards." Before a youngster can graduate he/she must pass a test on these basic competencies. No high school diploma without passing the test. Each youngster is tested after the freshman year, the skills for which she/he has not shown competency are worked on in the sophomore year and the youngster is retested. Skills for which there is no competency after the sophomore year are worked on the in junior year and the youngster is retested. Skills for which there is still no competency are worked on during the senior year and the youngster is retested again, hopefully demonstrating by that time sufficient competencies to pass the test and get a diploma.

Suppose, just suppose, a youngster passes all parts of the test after his sophomore year? He/she has demonstrated possession and mastery of all the basic competencies we say must exist in order to get a diploma and function in the adult world.

There are college entrance exams across all the

states which predict the likelihood of success in college. The tests are given "for all the marbles" at the end of the junior year in high school because it takes most of the next year for colleges to collect this and all the other information used in admission decisions. To prepare for the "real" test at the end of the junior year, many youngsters take the test at the end of their sophomore year.

Suppose, just suppose, a youngster passes all parts of the test after his/her sophomore year? He/she has demonstrated possession and mastery of all the items necessary to succeed in college.

There are "G.E.D. tests" given in all states which can be taken any time in life by anyone who doesn't have a high school diploma (General Equivalency Diploma = G.E.D.). A person who passes the test, no matter how the lessons were learned (on the battlefield, in the streets), receives a "G.E.D." diploma.

Except for the very interesting fact that high school youngsters would have to be dropouts before being allowed to take the test. Suppose, just suppose a youngster in his/her sophomore year takes and passes the G.E.D. test? He/she has demonstrated that the lessons have been learned which must be learned to get a diploma.

We say to the sophomore who masters the basic high school competencies, to the sophomore who scores well on the SAT's, to the sophomore capable of the G.E.D., and to the sophomores who can do all three of the above, "the gate opens for you in two years." That's yarn, very expensive yarn; too expensive for modern times.

"Ah," but you say to me, "there are many other things to be learned in the high school years besides basic competencies and classroom skills."

Ah, I reply, very true. But if you tell me the high school is the sole, exclusive place in which these other things can be learned, I must reply, "Yarn."

Whatever standards one develops and requires of all high school youngsters in order to get a diploma, these will be standards achievable by a great many of today's 16 year-olds. (I draw a line when I use the word "sixteen" only because most state compulsory school attendance laws require attendance up to sixteen.) And, if the incoming 14 year-olds knew they could get out the front gate at or anytime after 16, we would have hosts of adolescents working harder and longer to meet the standards; even if, and this is vital I think, even if we raised the minimum diploma standards applicable to all high school students.

The only people I know of who are sentenced to public institutions for a fixed length of time are prisoners and high-school students. We get very similar behaviors from both. Except, to prisoners we even promise that hard work and clean living will yield "early-release."

Now, once we get out of the Millbay Dock mindset about high school, all sorts of opportunities open to us through which we can improve our universal public education. Once we deep-six (throw overboard) the idea that high school is four 180-day school years long no matter what, once we cut that yarn we can really improve.

For example, for the example(s), let's look at the 180-day agrarian-society school calendar. I am sure we can all agree we are no longer an agrarian, farm-based society. We no longer have high school age youngsters working the summers on dad's farm. Mostly, these days, we have high school age youngsters doubling the probabilities they're going to get into trouble during the summer. Most dads don't own a farm anymore. Yet we still operate schools on an agrarian school calendar.

But, for the purpose of our first example, let's picture us greeting each incoming 14 year-old freshman. Picture giving to that freshman a list of the standards he/she will have to meet in order to graduate.

"These," we could say, "are the competencies you will have to demonstrate you possess in order to get out our front gate. You see the competencies listed there before you in math, science, English, history, art, etc. Over here, on this list, are the courses in which we teach those competencies. You can see in math as an example, Mr. Jones' course focuses on the algebraic competencies you'll have to have; Ms. Smith's course focuses on the computer skills required. In this particular case you can also see that you must pass Mr. Jones' course before taking Ms. Smith's. You can see over here that Mr. Jones' course is available four times a year; summer, winter, spring and fall; as is Ms. Smith's course. Remember, whenever you demonstrate to us you have mastered these competencies by passing the competency tests and are sixteen years old: you receive our diploma and depart the front gate."

In this scenario you can see Ms. Smith is working a full work year and getting paid as much as she was making at the bank. (I hadn't forgotten Ms. Smith.) Mr. Jones is working full-time also and not painting houses in the summer. And the students are working year-round also because of our next example.

Return with me to the scenario in which we are addressing the incoming freshmen. We had just finished telling them about departing through the front gate as soon as they meet the standards.

"Next," we could say, "is the listed amount of money, per student, per year, which the taxpayers have to raise and spend on your education these next four years if you remain in high school for all four years. If, however, you finish high school sooner because you passed the mastery test I men-

94

tioned, then you carry the remaining per-pupil amount with you as a voucher (since it would have had to be spent on you anyhow) to any post-secondary school or institution, or, or,—quiet down back there so nobody misses this part—or to any full-time employer who hires you and employs you full-time from the time you leave our front gate 'til the old-fashioned graduation date in June four years from now.''

You'd have to repeat it again to the freshmen were our scenario ''live.'' You'd have to explain that the average cost per pupil per 180-day school year in high school in your town and state was, for example, $3,000/pupil/year. A student receiving his diploma on his 16th birthday after exactly two 180-day school years had elapsed would have $6,000 of vouchers to use against tuition costs in any four-year college, two-year college, school of nursing, barber's school leading to a union card, welder's school leading to a union card, etc. Or, $6,000 to an employer who employed the 16 year-old high school graduate full-time for at least minimum wage from the date of front gate departure to the June date of a typical graduation (two years).

Just a note: At $3.50/hr for 2,300 hours per year an employer would pay out $8,050/yr. After two years in our example the employer would have paid out $16,000 in salary and gotten back $6,000 from the voucher.

Will this cost the taxpayer more money? Yes. It will cost more money to pay Ms. Smith and Mr. Jones to work the full year instead of the 180-day year. It will cost more money to operate the schools year-round rather than let them sit idle for three months, just like it costs more to drive your automobile than it does to leave it in your garage. There would be some tax savings, too. By having fewer students in school and by using school facilities the year round, fewer school buildings would be needed.

The actual per-year cost for a high school student in our example, for the full-time years he/she is in school prior to the 16th birthday, would be about $3,800; not $3,000.

This whole idea is far more complicated than my example(s). I recognize that and I am sure you, the reader, recognize it. The federal loan guarantees to Chrysler were very complicated but it worked and our auto-making business is healthier and competitive again with foreign car-makers. Our secondary school system(s) will have to become much healthier before they become competitive again with their foreign counterparts. A secondary school "bailout" plan will be complicated.

We seem to have a view that we should "hold" students in high school for four years. So pervasive is the view that federal statistics are collected which compare the number of students entering as freshmen to the number graduating four years later. We call the resultant number the "dropout rate." That's the Millbay Dock mentality, everybody is there for four years.

What, I wonder, would happen to the federal numbers people if a high school were able to report that zero of the students entering are still there four years later? I'd bet they'd assume the school burned down, fell down, had a name change, or, the federal form was filled-out incorrectly before anyone would ever think about the possibility the school was accomplishing its task in less than four years!

We are yarning ourselves, not others, about this one. Vocational education and math are two of my favorites. In math there are very few qualified secondary school math teachers. I didn't say very few "quality" high school math teachers. We are much farther in the hole than that. We have very few "qualified" math teachers at the high school level. At the same time we busily increase standards, require more "years" of math and feel proud. Problem is, we don't have math teachers enough to go around now.

In vocational education we invest heavily in capital equipment so we can train students in the ways of modern industry. First, we can't keep up with the costs of modern equipment, thus we cannot keep our equipment modern . . . the marketplace is changing so rapidly. We don't have computer-driven lathes, we can't afford them. We don't have robotic welders, gas turbines or the like. And, even if we did; and even if we trained our students to work them, the union contracts in the 80's are job-security contracts. An 18 year-old coming out of high school fully and completely up-to-the-minute trained is not going to displace the senior union member from his job. We're yarnin' ourselves if we think he is. Seniority is the deciding factor. And we hold our youngsters in school so they can't get an apprentice ticket (which is where you start) and begin building up seniority. Add to this the accepted fact that half of all jobs which will exist in 1999 aren't even known today. How could we train for them even if we had the money?

At the same time we are calling for more math and haven't got math teachers, the post-secondary four-year and two-year colleges have math teachers and declining enrollments. At the same time we are trying to train youngsters for highly skilled vocations into which they can't get, we hold industry to a high minimum wage for first-employment positions.

Instead of holding youngsters for four years and feeling badly if we can't, let's turn this voucher idea around and use it to our advantage. Let's work the 14 and 15 and 16 year old year around until mastery of competencies exist and then send them on.

By the way, and parenthetically in passing, when we were an agrarian society and school did let out so the kids could work on the farm, they did just that: worked. The idea that youngsters got out of school and relaxed, lounged, maybe worked part-time and played PAC MAN is a very, very new phenomenon; not part of our cultural history at all. The farms now may not be there as a place to work, but the schools are.

Then there is the king whose ego was so large he told the tide to "stay." We have entire communities with egos so large they create "mini-colleges" within their high schools to hold very bright children there for four years. The communities of which I speak don't pay $3,000 per year per student, more often than not they pay $6,000 per student per year. They pay that much because it costs that much to "have all the college coures in the senior year." They brag about their high school seniors passing all the advanced placement tests for first-year college courses and then graduate the seniors into the first year of college! If the youngsters are competent enough to do college work, as they obviously are, why hold them in high school doing college work? Why not voucher them into college for college work?

If a community commits itself to paying $24,000 (4 x $6,000) for the education of each of its residents between the ages of 14 and 17, then why not help that youngster go as far as he/she can on that $24,000? Not hold them back. Some of the scions of our industrial world who rise in the early morning hours and commute by train to work to assure no such wooly wastes of money and talent occur in business accept, without question, the very same waste when it comes to their own kin! It strikes me that at least some of these industrial magnates would cry, "Yarn!"

"Well, I know it's ineffective and inefficient," the industrial magnate will answer, "but without it our sons and daughters won't get into the high prestige universities."

Well, I reply, I've been through two of those prestige institutions: Princeton and Harvard. There is one characteristic of the people at those institutions which outshines all others. They have a nose for money. They want your money. They want your sons and daughters as alumni to contribute throughout life to the holy and glorious endowment. The prestige institutions will convince you the idea of competency-based graduations and community vouchers originated with them if it will keep your money flowing up the Charles River to their trust fund. If your money and kin are available and their admission system prevents them from getting both, they will invent the whole idea. (Or, perhaps, even a better idea; there's always that scant possibility).

100

How can a community, in this day and age of modern transportation and communication, take pride in holding the very best back? And while we're holding youngsters back, what do they learn besides college curricula in high school? Do they learn that hard work gets them ahead? I would suggest the youngsters learn just the opposite. They learn they're just going to have to sit it out, no matter how hard they work. So what happens? They start sittin' it out, of course. And while sitting it out they get attracted into diversions of the kind we all abhor, decry and do nothing about.

Again, I'm not suggesting we force the youngster out, ready or not. I'm suggesting we stop forcing all youngsters to stay. When the youngster demonstrates mastery of high school competencies, let him/her go on; help him/her to go on; encourage him/her to go on. Send him/her along with a voucher in hand for the money that would have been spent on him/her had we held him/her back.

One more interesting similie with the king and the tide. Besides using the Millbay Dock mentality to hold the high school competent youngsters in, we use the same mentality to hold the preschool competent children out.

Try as I might to remember, I cannot recall a single educator who agrees, in private, with the idea that all children are ready for school at age five (or six in some states). Chronological age is not the measure of readiness (which is the word used on the pre-school end, instead of competency). Some children have mastered the competencies needed for formal schooling long before the fifth birthday. The measure of school competency is mostly maturity, the geneological clock; not the man-made clock. Some of us mature earlier than others. It has very little to do with ultimate adulthood brains. Some children simply mature faster than others. Some early maturing children turn out to be average adults, some later maturing children turn out to be brains. It seems to be mostly heredity and some environment, we argue about how much of each in our business all the time. There is no argument, however, that a child who is competent is in any way helped by being held back simply because he/she has not yet reached a particular chronological birthday. To say a child is helped by being held back is yarn.

This is a real "Pandora's Box." Luminaries as brightly shining as Lyndon Johnson (with his project Headstart) have gotten bloodied on this buzsaw. Quite simply, it is very administratively convenient to admit into school on a chronological date. It is administratively convenient at the beginning and it is administratively convenient from then on, right through high school. It is not the best thing for the youngsters but it sure is nice for the school people. I've done it myself, for too many years.

102

I've said it to parents of four-year-olds, black parents, white parents, rich parents and welfare parents, "Yes mam, I know your child can read, but the state law is very clear on the matter, we cannot accept your child unless she/he has reached her/his fifth birthday before October first."

"But, she/he is ready and can read!" comes the plea.

"I'm sorry," has been my answer, "there's nothing I can do."

I am sorry and I apologize to all those happy, proud parents to whom I had to administer the first lesson in educational bureaucracy. I should have said, "Mam, we are two inches of boiler plate surounded by four inches of concrete which you'll never be able to penetrate."

We've even said that we, as a profession, are unable to devise a test with which to identify competencies. That's yarn. Give me a good, experienced kindergarten teacher and thirty kids and she will sort out the competent from the not-as-yet-ready in half a morning. There is no intellectual shortcoming in our profession when it comes to identifying children who are competent to begin formal schooling, it's an intestinal shortcoming.

Looking back on it from the clarity of a beautiful mid-ocean sunrise, I even had an occasion where I had hired and had funded 20 kindergarten teachers in anticipation of the projected arrival of 400

K-children (20 per class). School opened and the demographic boys were wrong (again), we only had enough children for 18 teachers. What did I do? I laid-off two teachers!

Why didn't I seize the moment and go get those parents of four year-olds to whom I had said, "No," during the summer? Why didn't I say to my board, "Look, now's the perfect time for us to begin our escape from this chronological age foolishness. Let's take all five year-olds and 40 of the four-year-olds whom the experienced and top kindergarten teachers tell us are competent? We can afford it, and if we start now, the word will get out and property values for homes in our community will sky-rocket. Everybody with young children will want to buy here." (When there's a strong real-estate interest on the board, use an argument to which they'll listen.) Lack of intestinal fortitude, that's why I didn't do it. Nobody else was doing it, why should I?

Instead of the black parents walking away saying, "That's Whitey for you"; instead of the white parents walking away saying, "It's just like the motor vehicles department"; instead of the welfare parent saying, "I could get a job and we could escape welfare if only . . ."; instead of the rich parents saying, "I'll go buy the pre-schooling"; they could have all been saying, "The school people care about me and my child."

Just imagine the parental support we could re-capture for public education if we did this as a nation. Why don't we? We know we should. The teachers are available. With declining population the space is available; but, all we do is yarn about it.

VII

THE SUPERINTENDENCY
(It Comes With The Territory)

Picture a hot sultry May Sunday morning. You, the superintendent of schools, awaken early and fix yourself a cup of coffee. You're worried that some high school senior in the district has, in the exuberence of pre-graduation celebrating after last night's prom done something foolish and endangered the rest of his/her life.

You, the superintendent of schools, take your coffee into your study and phone the police dispatcher. The dispatcher recognizes your voice because he always has the early shift and you've talked with him about road conditions on wintry mornings while deciding if the schools had to be closed. This May morning the dispatcher jokingly reviews the road conditions and then, in answer to your inquiry, tells you we've all been lucky this year. No reports of serious accidents last night involving teenagers. You, the superintendent, thank him, tell him to keep up the good work, hang up and relax with your coffee.

You decide to go down to the local drugstore and get the Sunday paper. Not wishing to awaken anyone in the house, you slip on the same dirty cut-off dungarees you wore Saturday afternoon while exorcising your frustrations on the lawn, pull the same dirty tee-shirt over your head, put the same grass-stained tennis shoes onto your feet and get into your car. It's early, no one will be around to notice.

The shopping mall parking lot is empty. You, the superintendent of schools, park your car in front of the drug store, get out and walk toward the store.

The rush of morning air as you're walking causes you to realize you forgot to zip-up your fly. Embarrassed, you glance around, no one is in sight. Quickly you reach down and zip-up.

In the store you greet the salesclerk and pick up the thick Sunday paper, there in front-page print above the three-column photo of you with your hand on your zipper is the headline "SUPERINTENDENT OF SCHOOLS EXPOSES HIMSELF DOWNTOWN SUNDAY MORNING."

That is a nutshell summary of what life as a superintendent of schools is like these days, in story form. It also portrays the press rather accurately.

This next is a true story. I once had a well meaning Board of Education whom I had convinced should pay their teachers more. The Board was balking because they didn't want to pay more money to poor quality teachers whom they suspected existed in among the high quality teachers they acknowledged existed and agreed ought to be better paid. No substantial salary increases would they approve until I could guarantee we had a system in place through which we could identify and treat the weak teacher; not fire necessarily but treat, through inservice re-training.

With the full knowledge of the union leadership whom I had briefed beforehand, I began requiring each building principal to rank his/her teachers, top quality to bottom quality and requiring the principal to explain to me, personally, what he/she was doing to improve teaching quality. To put teeth into the matter I assured every principal I was not going to recommend anyone from his/her building, most especially the principal, for re-employment until I was satisfied the principal was doing his/her observing/coaching job effectively.

Even though the union leadership knew, beforehand, the entire scenario I was attempting, when my "ranking" became public the union went berserk. I was villified as the devil incarnate.

One day, in the midst of all this, I was out in an elementary school doing one of my day-long observing/coaching jobs on a non-tenured principal. My secretary received a phone call from the wife of the six-o'clock news anchorman. She told my secretary she had just received a phone call from someone identifying himself as me and telling her he was in a motel room with a gun. If she (the anchorman's wife) didn't "visit" him in the motel, he was going to use the gun on himself!

Despite the fact that I had a school full of witnesses as to my whereabouts and activities for the entire day, despite the fact the reporter never even checked with me, despite the preposterous repugnancy of the story; the story ran in the paper "as is."

At least four respectable attorneys telephoned me and offered free services for a libel suit. Friends jokingly told me they knew the story was foolishness because, had it been true and knowing that particular anchorman's views toward "ranking," his wife would have urged "me" to shoot. None-the-less, that is a true nutshell account of what life as a superintendent of schools is like these days.

Shortly thereafter, someone put a bullet through the plate-glass sliding patio doors in our home. My wife was home alone. The police treated the matter somewhat cavalierly we thought, suggesting we arm ourselves. The press did not treat the matter at all, fortunately. I do recall a remark my wife made to me at dinner that evening while discussing the cost of replacing that large window if our home-insurance didn't cover it. With forced casualness she said, "Whatever they pay you for this job, it's not enough."

When it comes to superintendent stories I can truly say, "I've got a million of 'em." Superintendents with body-guards, superintendents being told they're fired while recuperating in the hospital intensive care unit from an on-the-job heart attack; the stories cover the waterfront.

"It comes with the territory," is the usual commentary when stories are told about the position. Well, maybe that's the case; bizarre situations do occur and no one should go into one of those jobs with his/her eyes anything less than wide open. But let's look for a moment at the "territory" one goes into.

Years ago, when I was closing out my Marine Corps flying days and contemplating a return to my engineering career, or passing that up for a commercial pilot's career, or passing both by for a public administration career, I went to talk with Arnold Perri, then Dean of the Graduate School of Education at the University of North Carolina. I asked him what a career in public school administration would be like. To this day I still remember vividly how the Dean (Colonel Sanders patterned himself after Dean Perri, I'm convinced) leaned back in his overstuffed raggedy chair and said, "Young man, a career in public administration in your lifetime is going to be the last place a man can have fun with his pants on."

To this day I truly believe Dean Perri foresaw at least the faint outlines of the changes that would happen in the 60's, 70's, and 80's. He sensed, at least, the population surge, the desegregation, the money, the feds, etc., which would make that old Southern saying applicable to the superintendent's job What I don't think anyone foresaw however was the change that would occur to the "territory."

No one could have predicted the shift which seems to have occurred in the general public's view of authority figures. It was a matter of "transfer" as some psychologists phrase it. A young population demanding that the perfect world materialize immediately, right there on the spot in the late 60's, had to demand it of somebody, and had to be told by somebody that perfection isn't achieved that easily. That "somebody" in the world of public education was usually the superintendent, in colleges it was the college president. Neither position has yet recovered. It's the old Roman story relived. The message was not what anyone wanted to hear, so the messenger got it between the eyes.

The authority positions of college president, school superintendent and many others, were attacked and degraded. Authority figures in general but public authority figures in particular, were not to be trusted; obviously, because they carried the wrong message. "Change," these authority figures kept insisting, "takes long, hard work; much more work than is involved in parades, demonstrations and sit-ins." That is not the kind of message activists in the 60's wanted to hear, especially those in the "now generation." Consequently, the public's trust of authority figures and respect for authority plummeted.

The irony of these times, as I see it, is that it takes the accumulation of responsibility and power into the hands of someone in authority to make change actually happen. And yet, people active in those times were busy happily destroying positions of authority. Even in the territory of Camelot there was a King Arthur.

Of course, it didn't help matters at all that we had some people in the very highest positions of authority in the 70's severely abuse their authority and thus aggravate the impression and transfer the view that all people in positions of authority were tricky at best.

The bright-eyed and bushy-tailed media reporters who teethed on "gates" of various kinds still remain convinced, I think, that anyone in any position of authority has to have a tricky, hidden, devious agenda fully plotted. It is the assignment of the annointed reporter to find a plot in everything a public official does or tries to do.

Hence the popularity of my little story about you, the superintendent of public schools. You couldn't possibly and simply have been fixing your errant zipper. There had to have been something devious behind the situation. Hence the villification of a person in authority who would dare to make decisions about others and perhaps recommend that someone not be paid from the public's purse for poor job performance. Hence the anonymous bullet into the harmless home of the authority figure.

The yarn of the times, in public service especially, is the idea that things can improve, that things can be improved, without someone in charge. We happily pass laws and regulations (ah—those regulations!) and then sit back and think we've gotten the job of change done. Hell, people make things better, not regulations. People make change.

Chrysler didn't change because we passed a law that there could be loan guarantees against which Chrysler could borrow. Had that law been passed and nothing else happened, nothing else would have happened. People changed Chrysler. In the public sector we just keep passing laws and creating regulations and nothing happens.

To think we've done enough by passing laws and creating regulations is yarn. Nothing is going to happen, other than what is happening in public service, e.g., massive debt accumulation, collapsing water, sewer and road systems, etc. We must once again recognize the age-old fact that people get things done. People with enough responsibility and power to make things happen, i.e., people with authority sufficient to make things happen.

Which brings us to the territory of the superintendent. The position of the superintendent of schools today reminds me of the country music story about the Arizona Ranger "with the big iron on his hip," with one exception. The Arizona "stranger," as he is first described in the song, has come to town to take the outlaw back with him, "Dead or Alive." "Twenty-one men have tried and twenty-one men have died," is the refrain. How then, could this lone Arizona stranger expect to succeed?

In classic story-telling fashion the outlaw scoffs at the stranger's invitation to return with him and, so, the stranger uses the big iron on his hip. Faster than the eye can follow, the outlaw lies dead on the ground, ready for travel.

The superintendent these days is much like the Arizona Ranger with the authority to act. Except, and this is the one exception, the superintendent knows he has no bullets in the big iron on his hip. He's not an authority figure, he's an authority figurine. He has oatmeal for support instead of silver bullets.

That, in a nutshell, is the "territory." We need not bemoan what exists, nor celebrate it at this point. It's sufficient to recognize it for what it is. The authority, the accumulation of sufficient responsibility and power to make change happen and, equally, to make change stick and take root, is

114

gone from the position of superintendent of schools.

Contrast the authority of the chief executive officer I've just described with the authority of the chief executive officer brought in to change the Chrysler Corporation. According to Lee Iacocca, he removed 34 out of 36 corporation vice-presidents during the first year or so he was the CEO of Chrysler!

Could Mr. Iacocca have succeeded in changing Chrysler if he had come into the corporation alone, with all of the existing vice-presidents tenured, with a majority of his board elected by and responsible to the union leadership and with absolutely no available money, not even federal loan guarantees? Of course not. Yet we expect school superintendents to accomplish change almost entirely alone into the very conditions I just described.

Contrast the authority of a school superintendent today, any school superintendent you might know or know of, with the superintendent in an Alabama County in 1916. In this particular county, the 1916 superintendent announced a plan to add secondary schools throughout the twelve hundred square mile county in sufficient number to assure every youngster (black and white) a secondary education. He wasn't announcing a 20-year plan, nor a ten-year plan, not even a five-year plan. Within two years of his announcement, that 1916 superintendent in arch-conservative, tax-opposing, government-leary Alabama opened the doors to 14 new high schools!

That's a true accounting, I know the county personally. That 1916 superintendent had the responsibility and power to make change happen in public education. Think of the number of children who have been beneficiaries of that man's action over the years since 1916.

"Extreme cases," you respond.

Not so, I answer. The condition of the Chrysler Corporation, relative to its foreign competition at the time Lee Iacocca took the CEO position at Chrysler, is the same condition our public education is in now relative to its foreign competition. The enormity of the change that happened in that Alabama county in the two years 1916-18, is the magnitude of change which has to happen 70 years later throughout our country if we are to catch up our youngsters to their foreign competition.

Superintendents of schools are not dumb. As I've said before, they are crafty. Cunning, some people would say. Occupants of superintendencies nowadays look at the "territory" and recite the "three years and away," joke. ("Three years and away," is intoned on the same musical notes as was used by the radio Lone Ranger when he used to say "Hi-ho Silver, away!").

The joke goes something like this. A superintendent, if he really wants to be a success in his profession, uses the "three years and away" management system. Promise everything to the Board interviewing you for the job, spend year one stretching the honeymoon, spend year two proposing a change and talking about it, spend year three looking for a new job and promising everything to the Board with whom you are interviewing.

Think about it. Wouldn't someone with an extra measure of cunning, who recognizes the territory for what it is and who knows he/she has oatmeal instead of silver for bullets for sustenance; wouldn't that someone act exactly as the joke prescribes?

I'm not suggesting we should, as the Lone Ranger's radio announcer used to say, "Return to the days of yester-year. . ." I'm suggesting we recognize the territory for what it is.

In the U.S. our public school systems are decentralized. About as decentralized as can be. There are about 12,000 school districts. That, coupled with a territory in which the CEO is an authority figurine, accounts for most of the reason why change, when we need it so seriously, doesn't seem to be happening. Ironically, a decentralized situation, coupled with substantial authority in the position of the local chief executive officer is the condition we had when substantial educational change did happen.

Parenthetically, the only power in public education which is nationalized now is the preservative power; the unions.

When foreign competition was out-producing Chrysler, change had to happen. With foreign competition out-educating us, change has to happen. Change didn't happen at Chrysler just because there was a need. Change happens when someone makes it happen; someone with sufficient responsibility and power to make it happen and see it through.

"Once burned, twice learned," is how the saying goes. During the latter half of this century we've been badly burned by people in authority abusing that authority. In the last few decades we've been faced by people in authority and told our high ideals would take time and work to implement; something we didn't want to hear. We've got media forms now which contain hucksters posing as reporters who promise us there is a villaineous, tricky secret behind every authority figure and they, the so-called reporters, can yellow-out at least three of the scoundrels for us in less than 52 minutes and eight super-suds commercials every week. Is it any wonder we place so little trust in public service authority figures?

There is a laughable irony about our media which I can't resist. Three of the most powerful authority figures existing these days are the three CEO's of the T.V. networks; hidden by the media from the public.

How then do we correct the situation? Interestingly, I don't think we do it by changing superintendents, or the type(s) of people filling superintendencies.

I'm reminded of the story I've oft-times heard myself telling boards who wanted to change all the school principals at once, in an upset-the-fruitbasket fashion. It seems a particularly pleasant and genteel lady's husband passed away. He was a banker throughout life. She turned to Digger O'Dell to make the funeral arrangements.

Digger obliged and asked the lady to come to the funeral home early to inspect and approve his preparations before her dearly departed husband's public viewing. The lady arrived at the funeral home at the appointed time but Digger was not around, he was late. While waiting for Digger the lady took the occasion to observe Digger's work on a body already prepared for viewing in the adjoining parlor. The lady was very pleased with what she saw, a well-dressed conservative looking body.

Then Digger O'Dell stepped out of the door of a nearby parlor, apologized and ushered the lady into the parlor from which he had just come so she could view her husband before his friends would arrive; which was by now very shortly.

"Oh no," she cried, "you've done it all wrong. My husband was a conservative banker. You've dressed him as a rock-and-roll hustler. He should be dressed in the same manner as the man I just viewed in the adjoining room!"

"No problem madam," said Digger, weaving his perpetually moving hands, "Just step out into the foyer and I'll see to it."

Digger wasn't gone 30 seconds when he returned and invited the lady back into the parlor to view her husband again.

"Oh yes," she said, "now he looks just as he did in life, with his conservative three-button vested suit. But, tell me," she asked Digger, "How did you make the change so quickly?"

"Very easy madam," Digger wove his hands, "I simply changed heads."

Changing chief executive officers every three years will not invigorate a dead body. As a matter of fact, changing CEO's every three years may be an excellent way to assure no change occurs in the body. In that short time a superintendent would be hard-pressed to accumulate sufficient power and support to make significant change, and to make the change stick. The emphasis in that last sentence has to be on the words "significant" and "stick."

In three years it's possible to re-organize the administration, re-arrange the deck-chairs so to speak, but make significant change, not likely. To make the kinds of changes suggested here will take time. And then more time to make the changes stick. Unless, unless the superintendent had something more than oatmeal in his holster.

120

With the kind of authority Lee Iacocca had when he came into Chrysler and the guaranteed loans; a superintendent could probably make real change happen within three years. And, most importantly, he/she would want to stick around as CEO, just as Mr. Iacocca appears to intend to do in order to make certain the changes stick.

So, changing superintendents or changing the types of people superintending is not necessarily going to get things moving. As a matter of fact, I've known some superintendents found to be making real substantive changes in year two who got the boot because of it. The boards, in these cases, had voiced commitments to change but all they really wanted were cosmetics. Friends of mine have gotten into situations truly believing the board wanted change only to suffer an early round TKO.

To begin with, we, the public have to face our own yarn. Changing the occupant(s) of our leadership positions as often as we do settles our worries about the possibilities for the abuse of power. Apparently, in light of our experiences these past couple of decades, we need to assure ourselves we can, in fact, overpower or remove from power the abusers. But, if at the same time we demand improvements in our public services, we are weaving yarn.

Also, we've got to recognize yarn when it comes to us from people we are considering appointing (electing) to our public service positions of authority. Promises of quick fixes to our public services is yarn and we must recognize it as such.

If, a decade from now, we haven't changed the course of free public education significantly; if, by then, we are still simply changing heads, our children will be so far behind the competition we may never catch up.

Suppose, for a decade, we put onto the state legislative books a law (good for only a decade) which allowed board members to vote no more than twice on any motion to employ a superintendent. Barring deaths, retirements, etc., the total number of times a board member could vote on the question of hiring another superintendent was two. Whenever a board faces the hiring of a third chief executive officer within ten years it ought to be pretty clear that the board has to be removed, automatically, with the governor replacing the board members. Again, barring deaths, or incapacitations, or retirements of superintendents, it would seem reasonable that a board could select a person that properly fits the local situation within two tries per decade. Otherwise, let's get somebody else in there to try.

With this sort of law on the books we'd have boards invested in the success and longevity of the chief executive officer. It would be a complicated law to write, true, but if we could write the volumes of whereases and whatfors it took to provide federally backed loan guarantees for Chrysler, we can get written a law that would cost boards who get into the cycle of switching heads.

By the same token, we'd need a law that prompted a superintendent to want to stay put and see changes through until they stuck. A law that prevented a person from occupying more than two CEO positions in the same state during any one decade seems possible. With this sort of law we'd have superintendents as interested in longevity as boards.

There are other ways to approach the authority problems. Some discussions have centered around seven-year minimum length contracts for chief executive officers, thus making it prohibitively expensive to keep changing superintendents. Some discussions have centered around tenure for superintendents just as there is tenure for teachers. I had tenure in New Jersey as a superintendent and watched other boards in the state routinely change the CEO the year before he/she came up for tenure. The net statewide result seemed to be greater turnover, not less. The point here is simply that the topic needs legislative attention and solutions are not beyond our ken.

Our system of free public education must improve. More of the same won't do it. We've got to change to improve. We've got to increase the likelihood that change will occur in a very dispersed public enterprise. People cause change. Frequently changing the people actually assures less substantive change in the corporate body, not more, because it assures no one person in the CEO seat can accumulate sufficient power and responsibility to make real change happen and stick. The belief by subordinates in a bureaucracy that "He, too, will pass," does not yield the kinds of change we must have during the next decade. We've got to put people in place, put them in charge and get on with it; and stop yarnin' about it.

VIII

BOARDS
(It Takes All Kinds)

Years ago (good grief, it's close to 25!) when I
was contemplating a career in public school administration, besides consulting the good Dean Perri at
North Carolina, I consulted the very best advice-
giver I'll ever know: my wife. She helped me to see
one very important point about public governance.
Until then, all those who judged my job performance were experts at the performance they were
judging. As an engineer, for example, my supervisor was an engineer of greater experience. As a
pilot, my check-pilot was a pilot of greater experience. As a superintendent, it's quite a different
matter.

It's a very important point I'm wanting to make.
I'm not trying to denigrate boards or board
members, but define the important governance role
they alone can, must, fill in our democratic scheme
of things. My friend had made clear to me a very
important fact 25 years ago. Were I to enter public
administration and become a superintendent, my
performance thereafter would be judged, not by
more experienced experts, but by amateurs; pure

rank amateurs. This clear and accurate fact gave me great pause back then. It still does. However, with all that experience behind me I think I can now see the beauty of it.

"Civilian control of the military," is what the government textbooks called it when referring to our Constitution. It's another unique characteristic of our grand experiment! Plain, average, ordinary, garden variety civilians, i.e., citizens controlling the experts. Citizens controlling the military, citizens controlling the educators, citizens controlling all the experts . . . what a beautiful idea. However did they think of the idea at the Constitutional Convention and whatever possessed them to think it would work? I'm here to testify, it works; given just half a chance, it works beautifully. It's scary to watch up close, sometimes downright frightening, but it works.

And! And (some of my superintendent friends will disown me for this) it works better than the experts! Civilian governance yields better decisions for the governed than experts' decisions. On many an occasion I can remember knowing exactly what needed to be done and simply bubbled with frustration that the damn board wouldn't see it my way and do what I had explained to them until I was blue in the face.

Looking back on those occasions from the privacy of my ocean, the boards were right. The route they chose to go was not as direct, not as decisive or incisive, not as efficient, but more often right for the situation than what I had advocated. Heaven help me, I can taste the salt on my lips as I admit this.

But! But there always is a qualifying "but" after such an admission . . . they were right when they functioned as governing civilians. Whenever they stepped out of that role and tried to function as Johnny-come-lately experts, they could foul things up faster than I could keep up with them. Experts are what they hire, governance is what they do; or, are supposed to do.

Therein lies the rub. Superintendents are not dumb, they are crafty. On many an occasion a superintendent will sucker the civilians into thinking like experts, flatter and otherwise con the marks into believing they know as much or more than the expert and get from them the decision-route the superintendent wants, i.e., the expert's decision. It's done all the time, for this and other reasons. It works but it's not civilian control of the military, it's not citizen governance of the experts, it's experts' governance of the citizens. It's not at all what our grand experiment has for a design.

If you find yourself talking with a board of education member at a cocktail party about an educational matter and he/she starts answering you as an expert, then he/she has been conned by

127

somebody and you're being yarned. If the board member says to you, "Yes, but children learn thus and so . . .," or, "The finances are very complicated and the critical factor is thus and so . . .," you're looking at a mark who has been smoothly conned. If, however, the board member says to you, "Yes, your view on the matter was raised and considered before we made the decision, as a matter of fact board member so and so holds a very similar view, but others hold different views and our decision was the best we could come to after considering these various views . . .," then you know you've got yourself a board member; somebody who is governing for you.

If you find yourself talking with a superintendent about boards of education and you hear, "Things have become so much more complicated these days, too complicated and too fast, I can hardly keep ahead working full time; how can we expect lay-people to keep up . . .," you are being yarned. Don't believe a word of it. If, however, you hear the superintendent say, "Yes, the board's looked at this situation from your view, and from other views also, they have differing views among themselves with board member so and so holding a view very similar to yours . . .," then you know you've got yourself a superintendent, i.e., an expert comfortable with the governance design in our grand experiment.

There is a story I simply must tell about how beautifully democracy works when given half a chance, a true story. It has to do with two small communities on different sides of a substantial mountain.

Each of these two towns, we'll call one "Brook" and the other "Ville," had been large enough to warrant an elementary school in each years ago. But, unfortunately, time and modern roads and big centralized corporations and changing values and a whole raft of other reasons had shrunk each town to the point that an elementary school in each was becoming difficult to justify. These people were (are, I'm sure) proud, hardworking, solid citizens; good families, good kids; no racial questions involved at all. Just proud as punch of their respective towns, but neither townspeople were particularly enamored with those people on the other side of the mountain; not at all.

The elementary school in "Ville" burned down (no one hurt), the elementary school in "Brook" was so old it was ready to fall down. The board had seized upon the opportunity to transport the kids from both towns to a large and underutilized junior high school building south of the mountain, an equal and tolerable bus-ride distance from both towns. "But only until you have enough money to build/repair 'our' school," the board was told. The parents from "Ville" told their kids to put up with those kids from "Brook" and the "Brook" parents told their kids to put up with those "Ville" kids until money was sufficient for each town to get a new school. The parents even maintained separate Parent-Teacher organizations throughout their "temporary" time at the junior high school.

A few years passed in truce before the State Legislature passed a school-building fund appropriation for the entire state. The signature ink was not dry on that piece of legislation before the two towns were demanding their respective new schools.

We scheduled a public meeting at the junior high school in the next available month. Each mayor, of course, wanted the opportunity to make his case to the board. They agreed that everyone would "listen" while I made a presentation on the idea of making the junior high school into a permanent elementary school situation for both communities.

A few days later an engraved invitation came to my home in the mail. The two elementary PTA's were jointly hosting a dinner at the junior high to precede the board meeting and Sue and I were invited. "My last meal before feathers and tar," I remarked. Sue immediately accepted. It was a superb dinner—linen, silver and pricelessly exquisite food; friendly people too. Although Sue seldom attends board meetings, she wanted to stay for this one; she and what looked to me to be absolutely everyone from both communities took seats in the audience. The press and T.V., of course, were there just salivating.

Each eloquent mayor, each parent president and citizens from each community spoke, in turn and civilly, to the board. "The board had promised and now it was time to deliver on the promise," was the message. Then the board president looked down to the end of the table, it was my turn.

My staff and I (my staff mostly, they were so much better than I) presented all the facts we could; the performance of the children now, the services we were delivering now, the performance of the children when last in separate too-small schools, transportation now and then, the monies involved in two new small elementaries, what could be done to the building we were in that evening with the same monies, the works; all the facts and all questioned until everyone was satisfied it was factual.

Then the board president turned himself and his attention back to the audience who had listened respectfully, as the mayors had promised, while my staff and I had presented. "O.K.," the board president said, "Now it's up to us to decide." He would recognize, in turn, each person who wanted to speak before the board decided. The place went church-mouse quiet. People spoke in quieter, serious tones. Democracy was about to operate.

I recall to this day the searching about and find-

131

ing Sue's eyes in the audience while the civilians took control and talked. Tough been-thru-and-seen-it-all Sue had tears welling up to the brim. She knew and spoke it to me through her eyes across the room. With us that evening were the spirits of ol' Ben Franklin and young Jefferson and all the others who had fashioned this grand experiment.

Before long one of the PTA presidents stood and likened as to how the kids truly were doing very well in school, her counterpart agreed and thought as how they had all gotten along just fine these past few years. The mayors extracted a not too hard to get assurance from the board that the total monies would go into improving the one building as would have gone into both smaller and separate buildings.

The place actually grew deathly silent when the board secretary roll-called the vote on the motion for one "Brookville" school and the unanimous result was greeted with applause.

Had the "expert" lobbied the board members in the month before the meeting, he might have extracted promised votes enough to have accomplished what he wanted. I simply sent the data early. I'm sure some board members talked to the mayors and other townspeople in advance. It was when they and everyone else realized the decision was to be for them to make, not an authentication of what an expert insisted upon, that the citizens grew serious. What the future was to be for their children was for them to decide.

A similar church-like quiet situation comes to mind when a board for whom I worked rejected my recommendation to seek a $26 million bond referendum and decided instead to seek voter approval for $40 million!

We all worked hard for them to gain approval of course, but secretly I felt they had been dead-wrong to raise the ante. Most other experts felt as I, even the self-appointed media experts. When the votes were counted the citizens had voted by a 3-to-1 margin to tax themselves heavily for schools for their children!

The concept of citizen governance of the expert does indeed work beautifully at times. The unpaid "Honourable Volunteer" serving his fellow local citizens as a trustee for the community funded public school system is about as uniquely American an idea as we have. But, the strains and pressures these days seem to create distortions.

Consider funding. The idea that the local community funds schools for local children who will grow up to become the next adult generation of that same community is mostly yarn these days. Funding, for a great many good reasons is no longer as local as it was for so many years.

State money makes up a far greater portion of the so-called local school budget than some ever expected. Education is a state function in our country and state support certainly is appropriate.

However, when the state steps heavily onto the scene, the state describes how their money will be spent. Nothing particularly wrong with that, it's to be expected. The point here is that the local honourable volunteer is as much a trustee of state funds these days as he/she is of local money.

And, with very substantial state attention to its education function, single-issue pressure groups can lobby the state legislators into including in the funding legislation specific requirements supporting the effective interest-group's single issue. Nothing particularly wrong with that either except, at times, we have the honourable local volunteer required to serve the interests of a group with ideas totally contrary to local views. The distortion of the local board members' original purpose increases.

Then there's the "beholden" board member. The person elected to the board by an interest group and who represents the interest group, not necessarily the interests of the community at large. This type of board member seems to me to be the most rapidly growing group, displacing the honourable volunteers.

This problem was portrayed when unions were discussed earlier. There is nothing constitutionally wrong with this phenomenon, nothing necessarily morally wrong with it either. It's just a factor of no small proportions which has to be cranked into the thinking.

As state level attention to education grows, interest groups must develop sufficient "muscle" to participate at that level. Some interest groups do, some don't and fall by the wayside. An interest group which does build sufficiently to become a factor at the state legislature level has more than enough muscle to be a factor in a local board election. With local voting in board elections, absent some major crises, running at the 20 percent level or lower, a well organized minority interest group mustering a bullet vote can elect one of its number relatively easily. Over the course of only a few years, such a group can build board representation far in excess of its proportional size in the community.

Add to this the political realization that such groups, with dutiful "yellow-dog" voters, can expand into other elections and we have the rise of aspirants for legislative seats entering and/or cutting their political molars on boards of education. Maybe this is good for education, maybe not. The point here is that it's different than it used to be. The political aspirant who sees his/her seat on a board as a stepping-stone, beholden to an interest group, a political party, a union, or whatever and knowing the support of that group (or groups) is essential to his/her next step, is a board member who functions quite differently than the honourable volunteer.

It's the old problem of Mr. Wilson and his idea, "What's good for General Motors is good for the country." Now it would aptly be phrased "What's good for the interest group is good for the children." As in Mr. Wilson's case, it's yarn.

There is another factor, born once again out of good intentions, which needs a few words. The so-called "open public meeting laws," however noble their purpose, have some interesting effects. Under these kinds of laws all gatherings, even conversations in some cases, of elected officials must be open. Moreover, they must be advertised in advance so the media can be present. Again, nothing necessarily wrong with such laws. On the aggregate, they've probably been helpful. But, there are interesting side-effects.

Federal money has the same effect. The board member has another "master" with which to contend. Every reason for every bit of money may be quite sound and of high moral intent. I'm sure it is. Distortion and stress, however, in the local board member's noble purpose and original local trust often increases. Local priorities may and in many cases are as equally sound as state and federal priorities. The state and federal requirements are seldom optional, they are musts. Consequently, the honourable local volunteer finds him/herself these days telling local constituents what they must do in the schools, no matter that it is contrary to what the local citizens want to see done.

A truly severe distortion in the concept of the local citizen serving his fellow local citizens as a trustee of their local schools occurs when a higher level government requires something of the local school district and doesn't fund the requirement. This sort of thing really stresses the local board-local citizen trust and bond. The board member, in this situation, must tell his fellow local citizens they must raise local monies to pay for something with which they might not agree at all. Again, the higher governmental requirements may be totally noble and the locally perceived needs equally as noble and quite different. The higher government's requirements shall prevail and it falls to the board member to mediate, not represent.

Let's take one example, the Mothers Against Drunk Driving. A very noble cause, no question about it. MADD wants youngsters taught the heinous results of driving drunk, at the very time they are learning to drive. The group petitions their state legislators to make such a course a high school requirement; which the legislature does. At the same time the local citizens are aghast at the poor performance of their school children on the National Math Test. They want math to be made a four-year requirement for every high school youngster. Another very noble cause, no question about it. Both noble ideas require time in the school day and no one is willing to fund a longer school

137

day or year. The board member finds her/himself having to mediate the situation, not represent the local perceived need.

"But it's only a few hours," MADD answers. True, very true. But add to it the numerous other causes, all/each equally noble (eyes, ears, teeth, reading, sex, etc., etc., etc.) and we have the local honourable volunteer torn, stressed and distorted away from the concept of the local trustee of the locally funded schools.

Let's add another reality. The idea of local citizens taxing themselves to raise local money to educate their local children who will grow up to become the local citizens of tomorrow. It's no longer viable. We are travelers. We move from region to region and state to state, job to job, snow to sun. Consequently, our local honourable citizen may not be holding in trust the education of his children and/or his children's children at all. He may represent a citizenry with a much shorter view of things. The present local citizen may simply want good schools until his/her children get through and he can move to a warm retirement location where, by some unfathomable twist of thinking, he becomes anti-school and anti-tax; as I mentioned much earlier.

Under these floodlight conditions, with every word public and reported, the idea that a board deliberates a question and the members, together, arrive at mutually developed conclusions is becoming yarn. In the first place, every one-member interest group knows he/she has a public platform from which to spout and get media coverage. With some unbelievably naive media reporters, the more bizarre the spouting, the greater the coverage.

Secondly, board members seldom can deliberate, in the sense that minds at the table are open to listening and being convinced to change. A board member changes his mind nowadays at great risk. What happens instead is each board member "has a position," pontificates the position in easily quotable phrases and behaves "heroically" by holding to his position in the face of everything, even reason. To do otherwise the board member risks public portrayal as "wishy-washy," or "undecided," or "standing for nothing," or worse.

The idea that a deliberative body considers all sides of a question, with minds changing because of logical, shared discussion, is becoming yarn. The noble drive for the public to see what is happening has changed what is happening. For a board member to vote one way on one question and another way on a related issue because he/she has changed his/her mind is deadly. For a board member to say, in answer to the reporter jamming the microphone into the chin, "I'm not sure, I want to hear what my fellow board members think before I decide," is the kiss of death. It's very mature but not politically astute.

For these reasons, changes in the sources of monies, federal laws and regulations, state laws and regulations (with and/or without monies for implementation), the premium on short-term answers, interest group muscle, political aspirants, floodlight conditions, and many more; governance by a board of honourable volunteer local citizens has changed. It's changed so completely and, I think, so irreversibly, that the view of local control by local citizens of local public education is a view that has become mostly yarn. We may lament its departure, we may herald its departure, whichever, so long as we recognize that local control, as a concept of governance, is now mostly yarn.

Ironically, boards may now be serving quite unique and singular purposes entirely apart from governance. For some they may be the last bastion of resistance against overwhelming amorphous big-brother-like state and federal governance. For others, boards may represent the first step in legitimation of a cause or a group. For others, legislators included, boards may represent a distant social issues battlefield onto which one can deflect or project political controversy; allowing the blood to be let beyond splattering range, then to embrace the views held by the victor(s). For some, local boards may represent the place where citizens vent their emotional discontent with all big-government. Absent these 12,000 "vents" the pressure might build to revolutionary proportions against unresponsive higher-level governments who won't live within budgets. For others, ranting, flailing and raging against so exposed and accessible a group as a board of education may be the cheapest form of therapy available.

It doesn't seem to me too great a generality any longer to assert that boards of education these days are mostly partisan. Boards are interest group controlled, union controlled, party controlled, state controlled, federally controlled and all of the above controlled. They are partisan. Partisan control of the expert was not the design. Bi-partisan control was not the design. All kinds of local people controlling was the design, and, it takes all kinds if it is going to work nowadays to change public education and insist upon improvement.

Don't, however, contemplate eliminating boards. The alternative is worse. Instead of two-inches of boiler-plate surrounded by four-inches of concrete, our public education would become surrounded by six-inches of armour plate. Nothing is as recalcitrant and unchanging as a public service of experts controlled by experts. We have no need to freeze our public education into place, we have a need to change our public education. We have no need to eliminate boards because they contain too few of the kinds of people extant in local communities, we have a need to assure that boards contain all kinds. Because, that's what it takes; all kinds. "Brook" and "Ville" changed because all kinds of the "Brook" and the "Ville" people were part of the decision.

How? How do we get all kinds back onto boards, or onto boards for the first time; whichever is your view? How do we assure the presence of business, retirees, unions, interest groups, races, both genders, et al.?

Gubernatorial appointments of board members was raised earlier. No one in public life is more astute at balancing and/or rallying disparate interest groups and the powers at work in politics than a governor. Ipso facto, anyone elected as a governor knows how to orchestrate hosts of different groupings. A governor knows an interest group partisan, a political partisan, a union partisan and every other kind of partisan, whenever he/she sees one. With five to nine member boards, each seat a six-year term, no one governor would likely appoint a majority to a board.

The additional item relative to board service is succession. Needed is a state law restricting service subsequent to board of education service. There needs to be a law which prevents board members from running for, being elected to or appointed to, any other public office during and subsequent to board of education service, for a period of at le⸱⸱ t four years.

This type of restriction exists for other offices now. We prevent a president of the United Sta⸱es from more than two successive terms. Many sta ⸱s restrict governors from more than two terms straight. Such restrictions are certainly not new. We could restrict board of education members from other public office, after board service, for a set length of time. This type of restriction ought to remove the political aspirant from boards, thus defining the service as truly volunteer and truly honourable once again. The gubernatorial appointee would, of course, still have to be a resident of the school district when appointed and during service.

Since board of education members are, in reality, no longer the trustees of a local endeavor but, actually, the trustees of a joint local, state and federal endeavor, then boards have to be redesigned to fit reality. Boards were designed to provide civilian control of the local expert. With deliberate structural redesign we could assure the civilian sufficient standing relative to the state and federal experts and continue civilian, non-partisan governance.

The target is a civilian controlling force which will insist upon improvement of the service and, if improvement means change, then insist upon change. It seems that we too often get from the expert only an insistence upon more money for the same product. We need a civilian element which will have the structural standing to tell the expert who insists upon more money for more of the same, "Yarn."

IX

THE END

Six months after "bringing the mooring lines aboard" my little boat, I returned to Mobile Bay, then the Dog River, then home. Two crossings of the Atlantic, two crossings of the Gulf of Mexico, and a complete traverse of the U.S. Intercoastal Waterway were not without effect, physically and mentally.

Physically I was forty-pounds lighter, my blood pressure was back to where it had been when I finished Marine Corps boot camp and my heart loped along at the restful rate of a long-distance runner's. I slept like a baby, ate like a horse and secretly delighted in wearing the baggiest fitting shoreside clothing I had.

Mentally, I had a far greater appreciation and love for family and friends, and a determination to be worthy of them. I wouldn't consider the trip finished until Sue and I attended a Sunday service conducted by the young clergyman who, at the insistence of a friend, had blessed my little boat before we set out. And last but not least, I had a far greater appreciation for this Country of ours.

We are so relatively young as a country, really only just beginning. We have so much potential ahead of us. There is no reason why we shouldn't realize our potential. We certainly shouldn't allow our free public educational system even to slow us down. In fact, education should help us achieve our potential; perhaps even lead the way. Other nations seem to view universal education as at least a necessary tool with which to achieve national potential. They would never tolerate an educational system that held them back or slowed them down. We can't either.

Not long after my return, Sue had occasion to take her new company car in for service and repair. Knowing it would be in the shop for a few days it became my assignment to follow her in my 18-year-old American made "bomber" and bring her home. "Land-life" was still so new an experience for me then that I was luxuriating in things we tend to take for granted. I had the air-conditioner in my old car turned on max-cold, the radio on max-loud and had extracted the payment of another ice-cream cone from Sue for the taxi service. As they say in some parts, I was in "hog heaven."

I realized along the way that Sue was taking her new car in for work while I was happily following along in an 18-year-old American car on which absolutely everything still worked. I began checking everything in the car within reach of the driver to assure the correctness of my conclusion. People alongside of me at stop lights just stared. The electric windows on my car kept going up and down, they could hear the radio on the down cycle of the windows, the overhead light, windshield wipers and window squirters on a dry evening, the electric seat adjustment; everything worked. When we arrived on the new car sales lot and I explained to Sue that my ice cream had melted and dripped onto my clean shirt because I had the heater running on a warm fall evening, I think she mentally added another piece of evidence to her growing list of suspicions that my time at sea had pushed me over the edge. While Sue took her car to the rear of the lot and the service area, I prowled among the new cars for sale; wondering which if any of them would still be around 18 years hence.

In short order a salesman was alongside. He was perhaps 30 and, strangely, his tie had been clipped off in the middle of his shirt. I asked and he explained that he had made his first sale earlier that evening and scissoring the tie was an initiation executed by the old-timers. The young man was justifiably proud.

"Aren't you Dr. Hunt?" he asked. I affirmed and he continued, "I thought I recognized you. I used to teach for you at such and such a school, for eight years. But I quit just this year. My family, I need to make more money. We had our second baby last spring. I taught mostly science."

I could feel he was hoping I would be understanding, which I was. I moved the conversation on to his family, looked with interest at the pictures he pulled from his wallet, told him about my trip and introduced him to Sue upon her return. He was very pleasant. I'm sure he's done well selling cars and is making far more money than as a teacher.

We can't have that. We can't have autos that take a back seat to the products of other nations and we can't have teachers selling them rather than teaching. We can't pick grapes and make wine for dinner tables on other continents.

Oh we can, sure we can. We can let ourselves become a sub-standard nation. We can let our human experiment become just another historical footnote. We can let our free, universal public education system help drag us down. We can even accelerate the descent. It's easy, all we have to do is nothing. Our children, grandchildren and great grandchildren won't have much good to say about us, but why should we care about that?

We can probably even yarn ourselves into thinking it's not even happening.